THE
CLASSICAL
COOKBOOK

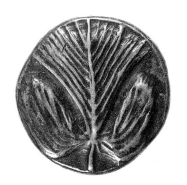

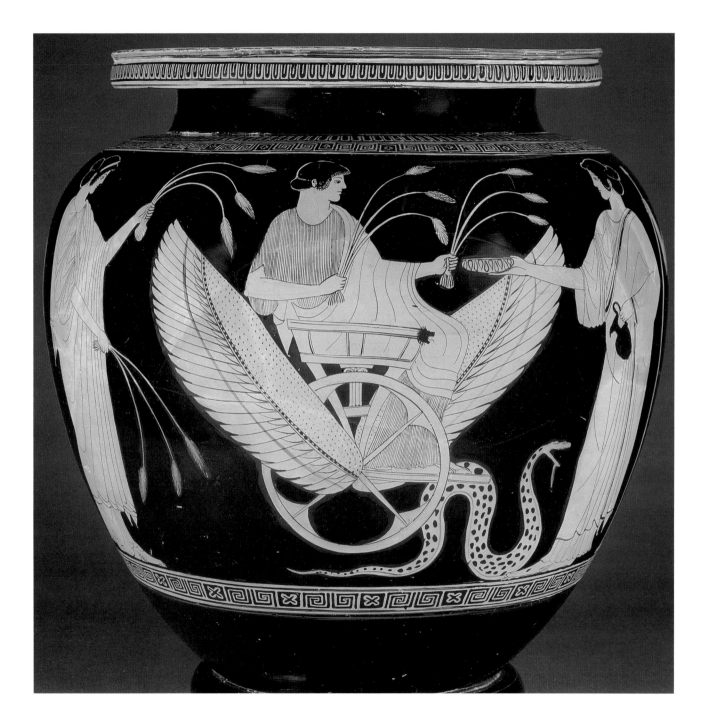

THE
CLASSICAL
COOKBOOK

Andrew Dalby and Sally Grainger

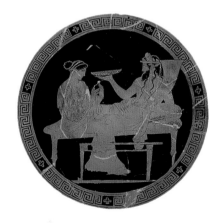

THE J. PAUL GETTY MUSEUM
LOS ANGELES

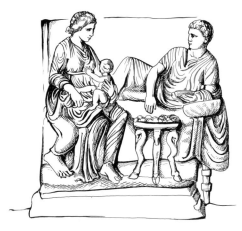

ABOVE: *A family meal portrayed in a relief from the tomb of Lucius Erennius Praesens. Lucius reclines; his wife and baby are at his side.*
HALF-TITLE PAGE: *The design of an early silver coin from Selinus, a Greek colony in Sicily, is a visual reminder of the city's name: selinon, in Greek, meant 'celery'.*
FRONTISPIECE: *Grain was the goddess Demeter's gift to humanity. Triptolemus acts as messenger, and Demeter's daughter, Persephone, offers a libation of wine as he sets out.*
TITLE PAGE: *Persephone, daughter of the harvest goddess Demeter, was fated to spend six months of every year in the Underworld as companion to Pluto. By a painter working for the potter Codrus, about 430 B.C.*

© 1996 Sally Grainger and Andrew Dalby
Sally Grainger and Andrew Dalby have asserted their right to be identified
as the authors of this work

First published in the United States by the J. Paul Getty Museum,
17985 Pacific Coast Highway, Malibu, California 90265-5799

Published in the United Kingdom by British Museum Press
A division of The British Museum Company Ltd

At the J. Paul Getty Museum
Christopher Hudson, *Publisher*
Mark Greenberg, *Managing Editor*
Lois Lyons, *Editor of the American Edition*

ISBN 0-89236-394-0

Library of Congress Catalog Card Number 95-082386

Designed by Behram Kapadia
Typeset in Plantin Light by Rowland Phototypesetting Ltd
Bury St Edmunds, Suffolk
Printed in Italy by Imago Publishing Ltd

Contents

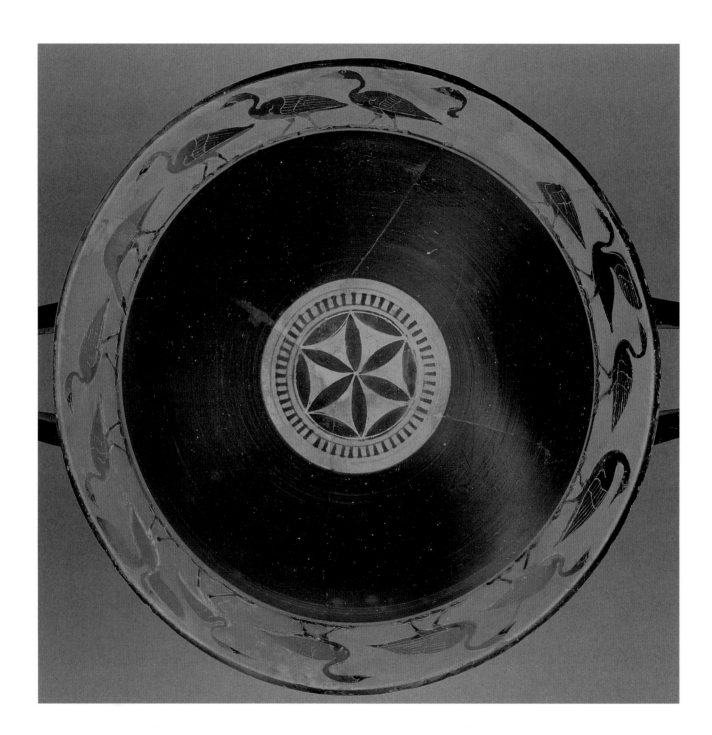

PREFACE

OPPOSITE *Half-filled, this early Greek wine-cup became a pool, with water birds patrolling its banks.*

We have tried to do something quite new in this book. Many people have written about the Roman cookery text *Apicius*, but no one has yet gathered a collection of recipes from the entire ancient world – from both Greek and Roman writings – and shown how they can be recreated in the modern kitchen. We have set the resulting 'menus' beside pictures and narratives of dining, drinking and festivity which have survived from that period. The result should, we hope, help to bridge the gap between modern experience and the tastes, smells, sights and sounds of two thousand years ago.

This book is a collaboration, but the reader may like to know that the 'I' who speaks about the finding and adapting of ancient recipes is Sally, while the translations and the historical background are Andrew's work.

Sally thanks the many people who tasted her experimental recipes and contributed through their advice to the final form of the book. Their honesty and frankness were invaluable in creating recipes that were both authentic and pleasurable to eat. Special thanks are due to Professor Barrie Hall and Annabel Hall, Terry McKay, Philip Hunter, Pete Whitby, Angela Dicks and Dr Chris Grocock.

Andrew thanks Jane Rowlandson and Gerald and Valerie Mars for their help, and Maureen, Elizabeth and Rachel for unending patience and support. The extracts from Philoxenus and Hippolochus quoted in chapters 2 and 4 are revised from translations by him first published in *Petits Propos Culinaires* nos 26 and 29, with the generous permission of the editor, Alan Davidson.

Other translations have been newly made. They are far from literal, sometimes adding a word or phrase to make the meaning clearer, sometimes abridging. Where quantities are given in ancient recipes, 'pint' has been adopted in translation as the rough equivalent of Latin *sextarius*.

INTRODUCTION

When there is happiness among all the people; when feasters in the house, sitting in rows, can listen to a singer, while beside them tables are full of bread and meat, and a waiter brings wine from brimming bowls and fills their cups: this seems to me in my heart to be the best of all.

Odysseus to his host Alcinous in HOMER, *Odyssey* 9

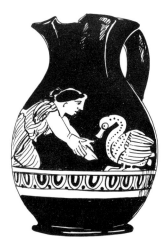

Ducks, geese and quails were all familiar farmyard fowl in early Greece.

The daily life of classical Greece and Rome, although separated from us by two thousand years of history, can be recreated in almost photographic detail.

On the painted cups and wine-mixing bowls of ancient Athens, vignettes of rowdy feasting and of everyday household activity are interspersed with scenes from the legends of gods and heroes. The wall paintings and even the graffiti of Pompeii, buried in the terrible eruption of Vesuvius in AD 79, allow us to see the citizens and slaves of the Roman Empire as clearly as they saw one another. From the garrisons of northern Britain to the fertile valley of the Nile, personal letters of unknown Greeks and Romans, retrieved by archaeologists, bring their writers back to life. And some of the greatest writings of the classical world were copied and recopied by scribes through medieval times. Never forgotten, they have become models of clear thinking and vivid narrative for modern authors.

These precious clues to the ancient world are not as easy to interpret as they seem. Not only were there huge contrasts between rich and poor; there was the divide between slave and free. The documents give us the chance to hear the voices, and see through the eyes, of all of these, yet it is not easy to put ourselves in their place.

One way in which we can attempt this is through the realities of every day. In any society, food and drink are at the centre of social life. A wealth of information is available on what Greeks and Romans ate and drank – in pictures, in written texts, in archaeological finds. In this book, therefore, we place real ancient recipes beside descriptions of household life and festivity from different times and places around the ancient Mediterranean.

Each of our eight chapters is based closely on Greek or Latin texts, supported by archaeological evidence. The narrative texts we use begin about 700 BC with the *Odyssey*, the compelling Greek epic of the wanderings of Odysseus. Our last major source is a conversation manual, written about AD 200 for Romans studying Greek: luckily for us, this little-known textbook runs through the dialogue needed for a leisurely visit to the baths finishing up with a hot supper (and with tips to the cook and waiters). Thus each chapter in turn takes a different kind of social grouping, a different occasion. Together they suggest the true variety of Greek and Roman life and food.

Immediately after this introduction you will find help with the problems of recreating ancient food, along with notes about some unfamiliar ingredients. At the end of the book are guides to further reading, including translations (where they exist) of the ancient texts from which our recipes come.

When the *Odyssey*, one of the two masterpieces of Greek storytelling, was composed, Greece was a land of isolated farmsteads and small towns, beset by wars and piracy. There were no big states: each little town had its protecting wall, and each country farm had its thorn hedge. The magic of the *Odyssey* is that its hero views this world as an outsider, for Odysseus is a shipwrecked wanderer, a beggar. If we can approach the world of early Greece at all, how better than to do it through his eyes?

Greece produced barley for bread, olives for the irreplaceable olive oil, grapes for abundant wine. But in that rocky landscape many Greeks depended on the sea for much of their food. Fishermen and seamen by necessity, they were beginning to explore the wide Mediterranean, the 'wine-dark sea'. In the centuries to come they would spread out and build new Greek towns all round the Mediterranean, at hundreds of sites that offered a natural harbour, a stretch of farmland, a route for inland trade.

Greek towns grew into cities, with the spectacular temples, theatres and monuments that are still to be seen, but somehow they held on to their independence. Cradles of local democracy, they led the world for a time in science, philosophy, seamanship and warfare. Sea trade brought the luxuries that were tasted at Greek *symposia* or drinking-parties (see chapter 2), where serious discussion alternated with music, games and acrobatic displays. Food and wine, the gluttony of fellow citizens and the self-importance of cooks were continual themes of comedy at annual drama festivals.

By 350 BC, when the gourmet Archestratus (see chapter 3) was searching the markets of the Mediterranean, Greek cities dotted the coastline from Spain and France all the way to the Near East. Greeks of Marseille were enjoying the wines of the Rhône valley, Greeks of Libya were exporting precious silphium resin to the kitchens of their homeland, Greeks of the Black Sea were pickling tuna. But they were losing their independence to the powerful kingdoms that now began to emerge. Archestratus himself, a Sicilian Greek, was a subject of the tyrannical kings of Syracuse.

Macedonia soon became the dominant power. It was from tiny Macedonia that Alexander the Great (356–323 BC) set out on his amazing career of conquest. Soon master of the old Persian Empire, he took Greek settlers and the Greek way of life to the Middle East and beyond, and brought back the marvellous wealth of the East. These riches, spent at lavish feasts such as the wedding of Caranus (chapter 4), caused ruinous inflation and social unrest in Greece after 300 BC. The scientists who went east in Alexander's time brought new foods to Greece: citrus fruits, peaches, pistachio nuts – and even peacocks.

While the Macedonian kingdoms spent their riches, however, Rome's power grew. Between about 400 and 50 BC this country town of central Italy, drawing at first on native resources (as seen in Cato's farm, chapter 5), became ruler of all Italy before conquering in turn Spain, Macedonia and Greece, northern Africa, Gaul (France) and the whole eastern Mediterranean. The wealth of the East was transferred westwards, and with the wealth came the demand for new luxuries. Inventive Greek cooks, and novel Greek delicacies, came to Rome. Chapter 6 draws on the hilarious *Satyricon* of Petronius and on other writings of the first century AD to sketch the heyday of rich and powerful imperial Rome.

The inspiration for chapter 7 is an invitation to a lady's birthday party. Found among discarded documents of the commander's office at one of the Roman garrisons in northern Britain, it combines with other texts to build up a picture of the daily life of soldiers and others in the distant provinces of the great empire. The Romans brought to Britain many of the herbs, vegetables and fruits that now seem native.

With chapter 8 we return to the great capital. In hot and sticky Rome the baths were favourite leisure resorts. In these luxurious establishments one swam, exercised, steamed, was massaged – and then one ate. In this setting we glimpse the food and wine of the later empire, inheritance of medieval Europe.

The life of the very poor saw little change over this long period. Bread was the staple food (barley bread for many Greeks, wheat bread for Romans), and some cities, including Rome itself, issued a free bread ration. Those who could not bake made varieties of porridge or polenta with their wheat and barley. For some there was *nothing* else to eat but bread, fruit and

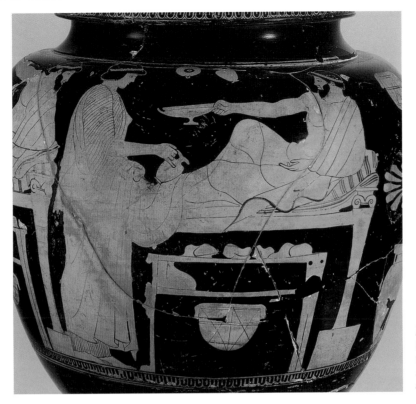

Food lies on the diner's table as he calls for wine: 'Copenhagen Painter', about 480 BC.

vegetables gathered from the wild, and such delicacies as shellfish and snails.

Even the leisurely banquets of the rich began with bread, however. For wealthy Greeks of about 400 BC the one main meal of the day started in the early evening (and drinking and talking might go on all night). At a men's dinner-party the host's wife and young children were never seen. Guests' wives were not expected, though some men might bring girl friends. Men reclined on couches, each with a small table; older boys, if lucky enough to be allowed to attend, would sit on a father's or friend's couch. A host would often hire a cook and waiters for the occasion.

The room would be lit with hanging lamps. Scents would fill the air, for perfumed oils and wreaths of sweet-smelling leaves would have been passed around. Both wheat and barley loaves were served in baskets. The successive dishes of the main course followed one another in a definite order, taken by a waiter to each diner in turn for him to select a morsel. They began with appetising savouries such as fresh fruit, shellfish, roasted birds, salt sturgeon and tuna, and meat delicacies in highly

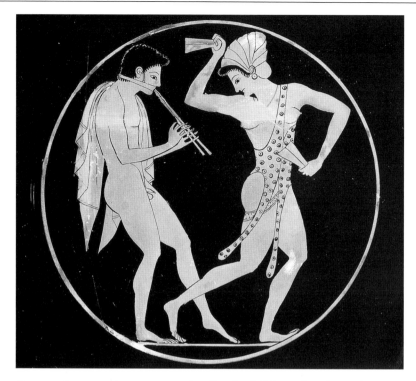

Dance and music, with double pipe and castanets. Vignette inside a drinking-cup, by the painter Epictetus, about 500 BC.

flavoured sauces; they progressed to fine fresh fish, and perhaps climaxed with stewed or spit-roasted lamb or kid.

Then the tables, with discarded scraps and bones, were cleared away and clean tables took their place. With the dessert course, known to both Greeks and Romans as 'second tables', wine was served. Greek hosts always mixed wine with water – it was a host's duty to ensure that his guests did not become too drunk too soon! The dessert consisted of cakes, sweetmeats, cheese, dried fruits and nuts: a wealthy host would demonstrate his generosity with a varied selection of these sweets as well as with a fine choice of wines.

The emphasis now turning to wine, the dinner-party became a *symposion*, a drinking-party. Sometimes the host and guests made their own entertainment, ranging from philosophical and literary talk to songs and instrumental music. Or entertainers might be hired, slave musicians, dancers and acrobats.

The dinner just described is the archetypal Greek dinner of history and literature. It is not typical of all cities, or of all times. This book will show how Greece and Rome, civilisations of contrasts, introduced endless variety on the theme.

These were not the first cultures in which attention was paid to the ingredients and the special flavours of food and wine. There are recipes on cuneiform tablets from Mesopotamia of the third millennium BC. Spices, herbs and vintage wines were found in the burial chamber of King Tutankhamun of Egypt (*c.* 1346–1327 BC). But so far as we know the Greeks were the first to think seriously about the importance of cookery as one of the skills or arts of human life. Professional cooks, needless to say, were in no doubt about that. Even Plato (427–348 BC), however, gave a few sentences of his philosophical dialogue *Gorgias* to putting cookery in its place. Around the same time an anonymous medical writer likened the work of the cook to that of the musician, in a passage of little-known poetic prose that makes a fine introduction to a collection of ancient recipes.

From the same notes come different tunes: from sharp, from flat; all are notes, but each has a different sound. The most different combine best, the least different combine worst: if one composes all on the same note, there is no pleasure at all. The boldest, the most varied sequences give most pleasure.

So it is that cooks make food and drink for us, creating dishes from dissimilars and similars. Now they vary the ingredients, now they use the same ones but with different effect. If one makes all alike, there is no pleasure. If one puts all together in the same dish, it will not be right.

The notes of music sound some high, some low. The tongue tastes food as if it were music, distinguishing sweet and sharp, discord and concord, in all that it encounters. When the tongue is attuned there is pleasure in the music; when it is out of tune there is agony!

Recreating Ancient Food

When you begin to experiment with ancient food, people will ask: 'How do you know what it should taste like?' The answer is that no one knows, and no reconstruction is secure. The recipes in this book, therefore, are a personal interpretation of dishes that are as much as 2500 years old.

Most ancient recipes present a basic list of ingredients with no indication of quantity. The method is often stated in a brief and confused sentence, or left entirely to be inferred. Even more important, there is no hint of what should be the dominant flavour. Fortunately Greek and Latin poets and agricultural writers occasionally provide clues as to how a dish looked or tasted and the manner in which ingredients were prepared and stored. These are invaluable aids to interpreting ancient recipes.

Cooking is an instinctive art. It should never be an absolute science, bound by precise quantities, times and temperatures. The recipes that follow should not be seen as the only way to prepare each dish – not least because the best ancient cooks shared this instinctive approach to cookery. It is no accident that the major Roman culinary text, the

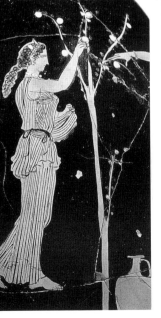

Picking the apples of immortality in the mythical Garden of the Hesperides. Small Athenian oil-jar of the late 5th century BC.

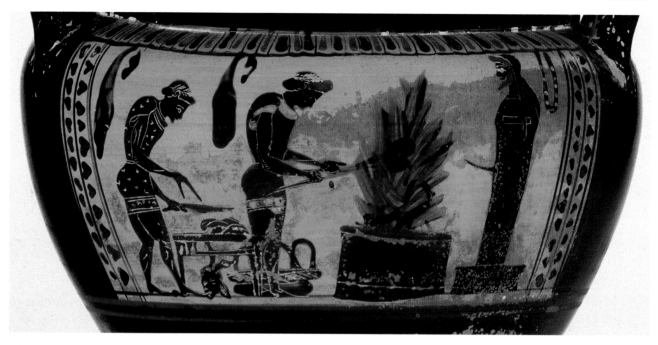

The act of sacrifice to a Greek god.

collection of recipes entitled *Apicius on Cookery*, gives hardly any quantities for ingredients. The book was apparently compiled for professional cooks, most of them slaves, to refer to as an aid to memory. They would not need to be told precisely what quantities to use: that would come naturally, based on their own tastes and those of their masters or employers.

The dominant flavours of Greek and Roman cuisine are honey, vinegar, a fermented fish sauce (of which more later) and a vast array of fresh and dried herbs and spices. The secret is to balance the sweetness with the bitter, sour and downright unusual flavours that appear in the recipes. The Romans (and to a lesser extent the Greeks) appear to have been unduly fond of sweet flavours in sauces. Honey and grape syrup appear in virtually every one. Wine and honey were mixed to make a sweet aperitif, *mulsum*, that was served at the beginning of the meal. This does not mean, however, that modern recreations of ancient sauces must be cloyingly sweet. Once you have developed a feeling for ancient food, you can imagine yourself, as a slave-cook, introducing a group of northern barbarians or provincials to the delights of this new and unusual cuisine.

Greek and Roman cuisines differ mainly in the quantity of seasonings used. The essential flavours are the same. The Romans are said to have

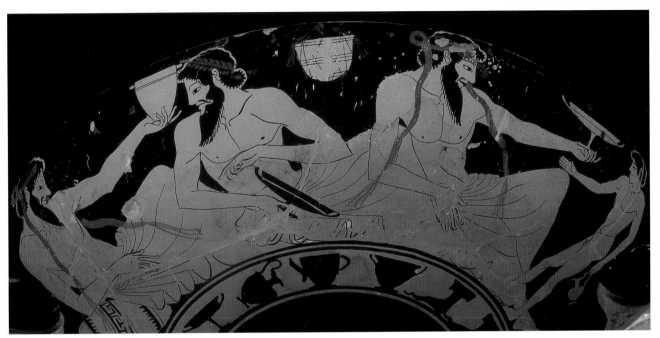

been 'porridge-eating barbarians' before they discovered Greek food towards the end of the third century BC. Eastern cooks, some of them prisoners of war, introduced the Roman elite to the new seasonings and flavours of the eastern Mediterranean. In this *nouvelle cuisine* of 200 BC honey, vinegar, fish sauce, dry and sweet wine, cumin, coriander, oregano and many other herbs were subtly combined to create a simple culinary style that stresses the natural flavours of the fish or meat of the dish. The Romans took to the new cuisine rapidly and developed their own ideas. Some Romans, forgetting the maxim 'less is more', developed a preference for heavily spiced dishes that were not necessarily to everyone's taste. Newly rich, they displayed their wealth in their food: spices were costly.

They left themselves open to ridicule and parody. A stage cook, in a comedy by Plautus (*c.* 250–184 BC), mocked this new trend:

I don't season a dinner the way the other cooks do. They serve up a whole meadow in their dishes – they treat the guests like grazing cattle, shoving greens at them, then seasoning the greens with more greens. In go fresh coriander, fennel, garlic and alexanders, and on the side there's sorrel, cabbage, beet and blite: they pour a pound of silphium into it, and smash mustard seed in on top: stuff so fierce it makes their own eyes water before they've finished grinding it. When they cook a dinner they aren't flavouring it

Drinkers discussing the wine. Below this main scene the 'Ashby Painter' (about 480 BC) has depicted a range of symposium paraphernalia: cups, wine-jug and the boots which guests removed before reclining.

15

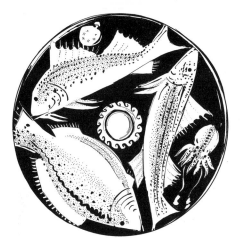

Fish-plate from the Greek states in southern Italy. Was it for serving fish? This one depicts (not to scale!) red mullet, sea bass, bream and cuttlefish.

with seasonings, but with night-owls that are going to eat out your living intestines! No wonder people around here die young when they pack up all this green stuff inside them, vegetables that are frightening even to talk about, let alone eat. If the cows won't eat it, you can be sure that people will!

Classical Greek cuisine added three or four spices or herbs to a dish: in a typical recipe in *Apicius*, as many as ten strong flavourings are to be found. Just as with complex Oriental dishes, the result should be highly appetising, for each Roman cook had to temper his recipes to the tastes and requirements of those who would share the meal.

Roman food can easily defend itself against any charge of excessive seasoning. The simple unadorned Greek style has its merits, there is no doubt. But there is something unique about Roman food: a taste explosion, reminiscent of Indian food at its best, that will be found new, exotic and exciting. The Roman Empire is often thought of as decadent and extravagant, and the *Apicius* cookery book provides some evidence for this, but it also strongly reflects a more refined, tasteful cuisine, a cuisine for the sophisticated, cultured Roman who had as much contempt as any satirical poet for the fashion-conscious gourmets.

Apicius contains such dubious delicacies as larks' tongues, sterile sows' wombs, dormice; a plethora of birds, warblers, parrots, turtle doves, peacocks, flamingoes; sea food such as sea urchins, porpoises, jellyfish. Other sources mention camel hoof and cockerel combs. They are all delightfully exotic and suit the stereotype of the decadent Roman gourmet who chose the most bizarre of foods because they were rare and expensive and fashionable, quite forgetting about the taste. By contrast we have concentrated in this book on foods that are available in northern Europe, are not too expensive, and are worth the attention of a modern cook.

These recipes deserve to be used and are intended to be used. They represent a selection of the best that Greek and Roman cooks have bequeathed us.

The Ancient Kitchen

Ancient kitchens are hard for us to picture today. However, archaeological remains and early literature both assist our imagination. The most striking evidence comes from Pompeii, where many Roman town-house kitchens can still be seen. This sketch therefore concentrates on the Roman kitchen.

The dominant feature was the hearth, which was constructed of brick and tile and stood at waist height. It had a pit to burn charcoal in the centre and a raised tiled edge. An arched opening beneath served to store the charcoal. A gridiron stood over the coals: on this were placed the earthenware pots and metal pans for cooking. The oven stood separately, often a low dome full of hot coals, which were raked out before the food was placed inside it. Portable ovens of metal or earthenware have been found, as well as the remains of baking bricks (*testa*). These served as mini-ovens that could stand on top of the raised hearth – or on a more traditional hearth at ground level. The bread or cake was placed on a tile and the brick placed over it; hot coals were then piled on top and around it, making a very efficient oven. Equipment for spit-roasting, and chains that suspended cauldrons over the fire, have also been found. Stone pillars in the centre of the room held wooden or stone tables for food preparation. Nearby stood tripods that would have held large mixing bowls and mortars. The mortar had grit scattered inside it, before firing, to give a rough surface for breaking down ingredients.

More elaborate equipment could be found in the wealthier households. Portable braziers that held a container of hot water, very like our *bain-marie*, have been found. These could keep food hot or even cook

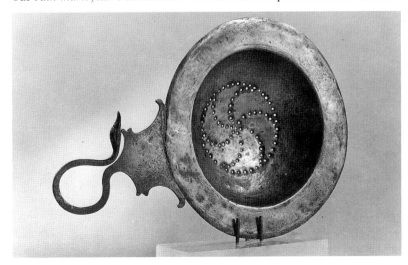

Classical Greek silver sieve, later prized as an antique by a Roman collector.

17

food at the table. Earthenware vessels for cooking were cheaper but had a short life-span and were difficult to keep clean if unglazed. Metal pans were expensive. They could be made from copper, or even lead. Cooks were advised to reduce must (unfermented wine) in a lead saucepan, which certainly increased the incidence of lead poisoning among the wealthy. A metal pan with a very modern appearance has been found in Roman Britain: a saucepan with lathe-turned concentric rings on its base, it allowed efficient even heat distribution without burning. Finely constructed metal colanders with elaborate patterns of punched holes; frying-pans with lowered lips to dispense the sauce, and folding handles; fish kettles; roasting tins and moulds in the shape of sucking pigs or hare – these are all common artefacts from Roman sites.

The atmosphere in these kitchens can easily be imagined. No matter how modern and well-equipped, a busy kitchen cannot be free of steam and heat. In those days ventilation was no more then a hole in the roof above the hearth. The heat must have been intolerable at times. Food was stored on open shelving, herbs and smoked meats hung from the rafters and amphoras full of fish sauce and wine stood around the room.

In a wealthy household the cook was a male slave. He might have many assistants, and command a certain amount of respect from his master. An eminent Roman will have wished to entertain in the most fashionable manner: his cook had to prepare the dishes that were 'in mode' at the time, no matter how bizarre. A poem by Martial (*c.* AD 40–104) depicts a cook who threatens to bankrupt his master with his demands for expensive pepper, and whose new oven turns out not to be big enough for the carcass he has bought. But in another piece Martial suggests that things went best if master and cook understood one another's tastes: 'Skill alone is not enough for a cook. His palate must not be a slavish one: a cook should share the taste of his master.'

Roman saucepan: a highly practical design, the rings on the base (right) ensuring more even heat distribution.

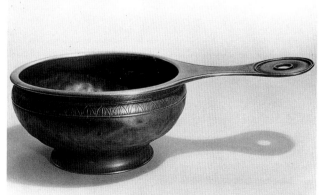
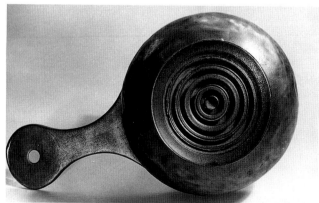

On farms like Cato's (chapter 5) the cook would often be a female slave, perhaps recognised informally as the wife of the estate manager (slaves could not contract legal marriages). Larger estates may have had a full-time slave-cook in residence or, as in nineteenth-century England, a cook might travel with his master to the country. For the peasant population of the ancient countryside, cooking was a shared task, but more often performed by the wife. City dwellers in imperial Rome, many of whom lived in tenement flats, had little opportunity to cook anything but the simplest of food unless they wished to risk setting fire to the whole building; these *insulae* did sometimes burn down because an occupant had tried to cook without safety precautions. Street food was, however, always available to the city dweller. Cakes and sweets, mulled wine, hot sausages and porridge, kebabs and all manner of meat dishes were on sale from street stalls and open shops.

The equipment and methods of an ancient kitchen would impart a flavour to the food which we cannot altogether duplicate. The smoke of the open hearth contributed an outdoor 'barbecue' savour. Cheese, herbs and spices changed and matured in the course of preparation, storage and transport. But some ancient methods have modern counterparts. Cooking on a gridiron over charcoal is not so different from using a modern gas stove. A pestle and mortar, essential for many of the recipes, are readily available from kitchen equipment shops today; they are useful for many tasks in the kitchen. A baking brick, the ideal accessory for reproducing many of the cake recipes, can also be found in a good kitchen shop: see under the recipe for Barley Rolls (page 53) for a discussion of the alternatives.

Many recipes require puréeing. A food processor is invaluable for this. Pounding and puréeing would have been tasks for a menial household slave in an ancient kitchen and would have taken hours of effort. If you don't have a slave to hand, invest in a food processor at once!

Some Unfamiliar Ingredients

FISH SAUCE 'Here is lordly *garum*, a costly gift, made from the first blood of a still-gasping mackerel' – Martial's verse, written to accompany a little present of a jar of *garum*, or *liquamen* as it was also known, cannot change the fact that Greek and Roman fish sauce has a rather unattractive sound. Whole fish was mixed with salt and left to ferment for up to three months. The resulting liquid was strained off and bottled. It was used – in surprisingly large quantities – in many Roman and Greek dishes. The smell given off during its production was so bad that making *garum* in urban areas was sometimes outlawed. Fish sauce manufacture was in fact the only large-scale factory industry in the ancient world. Archaeological

19

sites in southern Spain and around the Black Sea attest to the existence of a fish sauce industry as early as the eighth and seventh centuries BC.

These factory sites are, typically, beside a beach or harbour. The fish was only a few hours from the net when the process began. It is now clear that the image of *garum* as a rotten decaying substance is quite misleading. What took place was not bacterial action (which would have been impossible given the high proportion of salt) but enzymic proteolysis, a process in which the enzymes in the gut of the fish react with the salt to produce a pungent brine. This is why whole fish were used. By contrast, when the fish was cleaned before salting, the more active enzymes were removed and a clearer brine was the result: this was known as *muria*. The solid residue left behind when *garum* was strained off was called *alec*, and may have been not unlike the *blachan* or *trasi* of modern South-east Asia. It was valued in its own right for its seasoning qualities and as a medicine. According to an ancient encyclopaedia, *alec* was applied to burns, but it was effective only when patients did not know what was being used on them. Considering the powerful smell of all these substances, how could they fail to guess?

It is quite clear from the ancient recipes that *garum*, or *liquamen*, was a strongly flavoured brine, thin and free-flowing. Amphoras labelled 'best strained *liquamen*' have been found. Roman fish sauce was absolutely nothing like modern anchovy paste: using the latter has been the downfall of many an attempt to recreate ancient recipes.

Enthusiasts for Roman food have tried to make *garum* in modern Britain and North America. Unless carried out under a hot sun and at a considerable distance from neighbours, these experiments are unwise and probably unsafe. Luckily there is no need for them. Fish sauce was utterly indispensable in ancient cookery (it is the way in which salt was added to nearly every recipe), but it is also essential, to this day, to the cuisine of South-east Asia. In modern South-east Asia the making of fish sauce, by a month-long fermentation process almost identical with what is described in the ancient sources, is a widespread cottage industry.

When setting out to recreate ancient flavours, then, you must start with a bottle of fish sauce, Vietnamese *nuoc mam* or Thai *nam pla*. There are health questions concerning the unpasteurised fish sauces marketed in South-east Asia itself, but the brands that are exported are pasteurised, and this treatment makes no real difference to the flavour of the finished dish. *Nuoc mam* can be bought in any Chinese supermarket. If you cannot find a local source, ask for advice from the nearest Thai or Vietnamese restaurant.

Incidentally, there are from time to time rumours that *garum*-making has survived at this or that Mediterranean village. As far as Greece and Italy are concerned, these are nothing more than rumours so far. In ancient times fish sauce was often infused with herbs during preparation. I always decant my *nuoc man* and add fresh sprigs of oregano or rue.

SILPHIUM AND ASAFOETIDA Silphium was a remarkable spice, known to Greeks and Romans for its medicinal properties as well as for its use in food. It was grown only in Cyrenaica (modern Libya) and was so valuable that the Roman state treasury stored it alongside gold and silver. Then came a disaster for the history of cuisine. The Roman encyclopaedist Pliny (AD 24–79) explains that silphium was no longer to be found:

For many years now it has not been seen in Libya: the agents who lease grazing land, scenting higher profits, had allowed sheep to overgraze the silphium stands. The single stem found within living memory was sent to the Emperor Nero. If an animal should ever come upon a promising shoot, the sign will be that a sheep after eating it rapidly goes to sleep, whereas a goat sneezes rather loudly. For a long time now, however, the only silphium brought to us in Rome has been that originating in Iran and Armenia, which is plentiful enough, but not nearly as good as Cyrenaic.

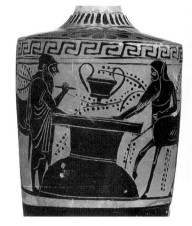

Two centaurs taste the new wine. It was fermented in huge half-sunken earthenware vats (pithoi).

Scholars have found it hard to believe that the silphium of Libya could really have become extinct, and you sometimes read of its rediscovery. But the goat never sneezes: the rediscovered 'silphium' never has the flavour or the power of its legendary forebear. Nero really did eat the last of it.

Luckily the substitute that was used from Pliny's time onwards, the 'silphium' of Central Asia, is still easily available, although it is hardly ever used by Western cooks. It is asafoetida, the resin of the plant *Ferula asafoetida*, a relative of fennel. In using this we can be confident that we are doing exactly what the cooks of the Roman Empire, the cooks who first used the recipes of *Apicius*, would have done. Asafoetida is used widely in the Middle East for medicinal purposes, and in India in cookery (it is often listed as an ingredient on packets of ready-made poppadoms and nans). It is rumoured to be one of the secret ingredients in Worcestershire Sauce. The pure aroma and flavour of asafoetida can be compared with leek or garlic, but are best signalled by one of its modern names, 'devil's dung'.

Asafoetida can be purchased in the West in two different forms, both deriving from the resin that is tapped from the root of the plant. We prefer the pure tincture, wonderfully rich and pungent. Once widely available from chemists, it can still be bought from a well-stocked apothecary or herbalist. Baldwin's (for the address see page 24) can provide this as well as many of the obscure herbs called for in ancient recipes. Almost as powerful is the asafoetida that is sold as *hing* in Indian

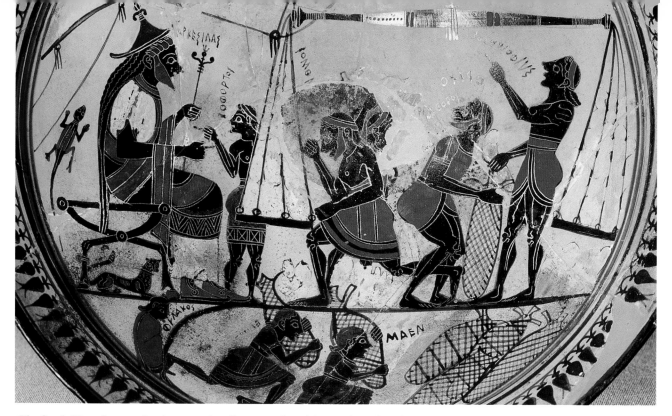

The Greek King of Cyrene (modern Libya) supervising exports. This 6th-century-BC Spartan cup is said to depict the silphium business, a Cyrenaic monopoly.

food stores. A yellow powder, this consists of asafoetida resin mixed with flour or bean meal to stabilise it, just as was done with ancient silphium; turmeric may also be added for colour.

The recipes that follow suggest the quantity of asafoetida to use, whether a pinch of *hing* or one or two drops of tincture. Whichever form you use, take care. Asafoetida can impart a particularly unpleasant taste when used to excess, as I found to my cost during my early experiments. For a Roman banquet for seventy people, I made half a gallon of lentil stew which I unfortunately seasoned with rather too much asafoetida. In an attempt to salvage the stew I added honey. This worked, but it needed too much honey. As a last resort I added sugar, which saved the dish and turned it into a success. Sugar was a costly rarity in ancient Rome – a medicine, not a food ingredient – but my situation was desperate!

LOVAGE This, *Levisticum officinale*, is the single most commonly used herb in *Apicius*. There are at least fifty recipes that begin with the words 'pound pepper and lovage'. Romans used it at least as commonly as a modern cook might use parsley. It has a bitter sharp flavour that has perhaps caused it to lose popularity in recent centuries, yet it is very useful in everyday cooking, and especially good in fish and pulse (legume) dishes. Its flavour is fundamental to authentic Roman food.

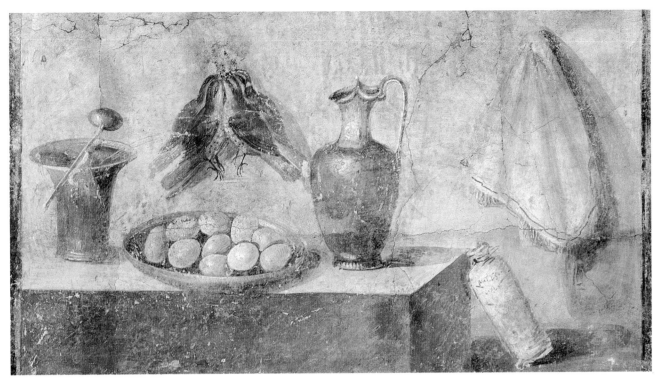

Lovage grows well in a temperate climate and it is best used fresh. If you have a herb garden, give it a try – but remember that it can reach 10 ft (3 m). If your supply runs out, however, you can use the pale green leaves of celery as an alternative: the flavour is remarkably similar. If you have access to a large supply of lovage all at once, you can preserve it by chopping it finely and storing it in olive oil.

RUE Another culinary herb that was once very popular, *Ruta graveolens* is now rarely used. This is a pity: its unusual bitter flavour is still valuable in the kitchen, and it has had a great reputation as a medicinal herb. It, too, imparts an unmistakable flavour to ancient recipes.

Rue is a hardy evergreen that grows well in any soil. It can be found dried, but it is so easily grown – even on the window sill – that the dried leaf need never be used. The stems and leaves of rue can cause an allergic reaction in sensitive skins if picked in bright sunlight, so take care over this. Once picked, it is quite safe as a food ingredient.

OTHER HERBS AND SPICES The vast majority of herbs and spices mentioned in this book are readily available from herbalists, health-food shops and supermarkets (aniseed, fennel seed, pine kernels, poppy seed). Most of the herbs can be grown in any garden (pennyroyal, for

Still-life from the House of Julia Felix, Pompeii: a tasselled cloth, a pewter wine-jug, thrushes, a plate of eggs, a small jar of wine, and a bronze mortar and serving spoon all help to suggest luxury food and wine.

23

example). Calamint is not so easy to find, unless you know where it grows wild. Bay berries can be picked in late winter or early spring if you have a bay tree, or they can sometimes be found on fresh bay leaves when you buy them. 'Bitter almonds' found in a Chinese supermarket, though not the same species as ancient bitter almonds, are a safer substitute for them, because the bitter variety of our western almond is poisonous unless roasted. Ground coriander seed is widely available; coriander leaf is not so common. The plant will not grow everywhere, but fresh coriander is sold in season in bunches in many food stores. It can also be bought preserved in oil, as described for lovage above.

A good mail-order source of unusual herbs and spices in the UK is G. Baldwin & Co. Ltd, 171–173 Walworth Road, London SE17 1RW.

PASSUM (RAISIN WINE) 'A Knossos vine, out of Minoan Crete, sends you this raisin wine. It is the poor man's usual *Mulsum*,' wrote Martial. The Romans used many different types of sweetener in their sauces, one of the finest of which was *passum*, which also imparted a rich deep colour. Raisin wine was made in Crete throughout ancient and medieval times, and is still produced in Italy and France (where it is known as *vin de paille*). It is certainly not a poor man's drink. The poet Martial's little gift-verse, quoted above, is displaying false modesty. For more on *mulsum*, incidentally, see the recipe for Spiced Wine on page 101.

Pliny describes how the Cretans made their famous raisin wine:

Some make *passum* from any sweet, early-ripening, white grapes, drying the bunches in the sun till little over half their weight remains. Then they gently express the must. The more painstaking makers dry the grapes in this same way, pick the individual grapes and soak them, without the stalks, in fine wine till they swell, and *then* press them. This style is considered better than any other.

You may be understandably reluctant to buy expensive *passito*, or *vin santo*, modern raisin wine, from an Italian food store, for use as a food flavouring; indeed, you may not be able to find them. Luckily the Latin farming writer Columella (*c.* AD 60) gives full instructions for making *passum*, from which it is clear that a version adequate for cooking, based on red wine, can be imitated on a small scale in the modern kitchen. Take 1 pint (2½ cups/570 ml) red wine and 4 oz (120 g) raisins. Soak the raisins in the wine for two to three days until they are soft and swollen. Blend or mash the mixture and strain through a fine sieve, pushing through as much as possible of the pulp. The result can be used immediately.

DEFRUTUM AND OTHER CONCENTRATED GRAPE JUICES *Caroenum, defrutum* and *sapa* were grape musts reduced by boiling. Like *passum* they

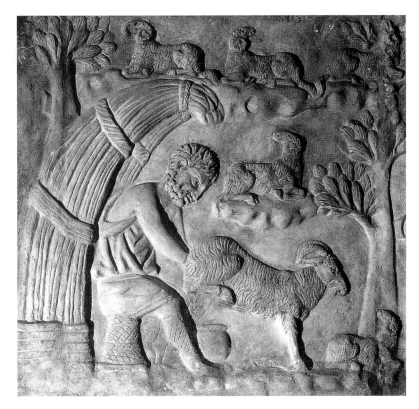

Farmer milking a goat. Roman tomb relief.

were used as sweeteners in sauces. The three names identify different strengths. *Defrutum*, which is needed in some of the recipes in this book, is red grape juice reduced by a half or more. Simply take 1 litre (4⅓ cups) red grape juice, reduce it until one third is left, and store. It is used in tablespoon measures.

ANCIENT AND MODERN CHEESES Greeks and Romans made many different types of cheese, but there is little detailed information about them. Most of the recipes simply call for goat's or sheep's cheese (cow's milk cheese is not so often required), without telling us what the texture was. Yet the texture is all-important for the recipes in this book, particularly for the sweet cakes from Cato's farming handbook in chapter 5. Here fresh cheese is essential, because new cheese has little saltiness to interfere with the honey.

Columella gives useful instructions for cheese-making. He tells us to put a pennyweight of rennet, the weight of a silver denarius (⅘ oz/23 g), to a gallon (1¼ US gallons/4.5 litres) of milk. The milk is then warmed and, when it begins to curdle, is strained through a wicker basket. It is then moulded and compressed. At this stage it can either be hardened with salt or simply soaked briefly in brine.

I wanted to make a soft sweet cheese to use in the recipe for Layered Cheesecake (page 94), and in following Columella's instructions tried to keep the salt to a minimum. It was very successful as an eating cheese, but unfortunately not suitable for the cheesecake. Having experimented with many different cheeses, I recommend feta, a type which dates from medieval times and may be made from either sheep's or goat's milk; chèvre, a goat's milk cheese also known as boucheron, that is sold in the traditional log shape; Pecorino Romano, a hard sheep's cheese very similar to Parmesan; ricotta, which is traditionally made from the whey left over from the manufacture of Pecorino Romano; and Pecorino Toscano, a semi-hard sheep's cheese that is mildly salty and is the closest I can find to the cheese I myself made using Columella's recipe.

A NOTE ABOUT BRAINS AND SWEETBREADS Greeks and Romans used these frequently in their stuffings and sausages. They are included in the recipes that follow, but obviously using them is a matter of individual choice. In Britain BSE (bovine spongiform encephalopathy), commonly known as 'mad cow disease', is still widespread in cattle and it will be a long time before the disease has been eradicated; and the possible link with human Kreutzfeld-Jakob disease has not been disproved. For this reason calf's brain must not be used in Britain. Officially lamb's brain and sweetbreads are said to be safe, yet they have become very scarce because of the prevailing caution. An independent butcher may be able to obtain them. Sweetbreads are delicious and it is a great pity that they have become so unpopular. Lamb's brain, as used in Roman stuffing, is also strongly recommended. In the two recipes in which it occurs I have suggested minced (ground) lamb as an alternative.

MEASURES used in the recipes are level unless otherwise stated.

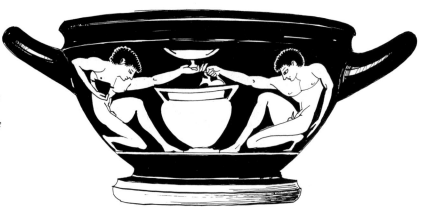

How to serve wine, Athenian style. Wine is already mixed with water in the krater: *the* oinochoe *(jug) is dipped into the* krater *in order to fill the cups (two kinds*, skyphos *and* kylix*) held by the boy on the left.*

I

THE HOMECOMING
OF ODYSSEUS

The ten-year siege of Troy, the victory gained by means of a wooden horse, the unhappy homecomings of the victorious Greek warriors – these stories were familiar to every Greek who went to school. They were told in the *Iliad* and *Odyssey*, two epic tales which, as everyone knew, had been sung by a blind poet, Homer, before recorded history began. They were tales so marvellous that nothing could spoil them, not even the fact that they were set texts to be learnt by heart.

Homer himself did not say how many hundreds of years had passed since Troy fell: he was singing of a lost age of heroes. Now that Troy and Mycenae and Pylos have been excavated we know that if the siege ever happened, as the *Iliad* tells us it did, it must have been before 1200 BC, five centuries or more before the poems were composed.

In the *Iliad* and *Odyssey* a whole world is pictured. It is not the real Mycenaean world of 1300 BC with its labyrinthine palaces and its clay tablets; nor is it quite the Greek world of 700 BC in which Homer must have lived. But it is a world so convincing in every detail, and so familiar to all who read the epics, that it has to be part of any reconstruction of Greek and Roman life.

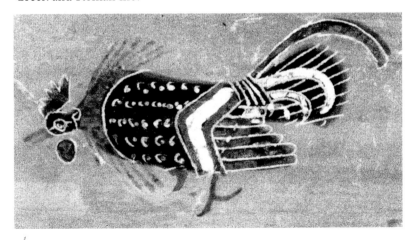

A fighting-cock: early evidence of the introduction of the domestic chicken to Greece, on an Athenian cup of about 450 BC, probably by the 'Tleson Painter'.

27

The *Iliad* tells the story of the Greek warriors' quarrels outside the walls of Troy. There they raided or hunted for meat. And with their roast meat they drank strong, sweet, red wine, brought there by seamen who would beach their ships, set up a market on the shore and accept captive slaves and livestock in exchange for their vintage.

In the *Odyssey* we hear of Odysseus' ten-year wanderings and adventures on his way home to Ithaca. He stayed too long, perhaps, with the beautiful goddess Calypso, till Hermes, the gods' messenger, came to tell her that it was time to let him go. The poet shows us Calypso and Odysseus sharing a homely supper before going to bed together for the last time: 'They came to the hollow cave, the goddess and the man together. So he was sitting there on the chair where Hermes had sat, and the young woman laid out every food, for him to eat and drink, that mortal men can eat; she was sitting facing godlike Odysseus, and maids put out ambrosia and nectar for her.'

It is part of the charm of the *Odyssey* that a picture of a young housewife, serving her man with food before eating herself, can the next moment be a portrait of a goddess attended by maids – for it was immortals who had to feed on ambrosia and nectar.

Shipwrecked on Scherie (a fantasy island, but believed by many to be Corfu), Odysseus was fortunate to be welcomed to the palace of Alcinous. He paused to admire the king's fruit garden: 'Outside the yard is a big orchard on both sides of the gates, of four acres, and a hedge runs along each side of it. There, tall trees spread their leaves, pears and pomegranates and shiny-fruited apples and sweet figs and leafy olives. Their fruit never fails or falls short, winter or summer, all the year: as the West Wind blows it fertilises some and ripens others. Pear upon pear grows old and apple upon apple, grapes upon grapes and fig upon fig.'

Food and drink were at the centre of Homeric life. Food left over from the last meal was, by unspoken rule, given generously to a stranger before he was asked his name. And in a king's household, lavish feasting was the order of the day even when the king himself was missing and feared dead.

This, at all events, was what Odysseus discovered when he returned to his homeland of Ithaca. Disguised as a penniless vagrant, carrying a leather begging bag which he hoped to fill with food, drawn by the smell of roast meat (beef, mutton or pork would have been roasted over an open fire in the farmyard), Odysseus stood at last at the doorway of his own smoke-filled hall, watching the carousal of the men who were competing to claim the hand of his faithful Penelope.

At the central fireplace of a Homeric household, we gather, the women, children and servants clustered. Men sat on stools around the walls, each with a well-scrubbed table before him. The tables had to be clean, for the diners had no plates. Joints of roast meat were served, bread

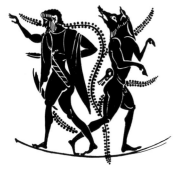

Odysseus is not affected by Circe's magic potion. His men were not so lucky and have been turned into swine (see page 40). 'Daybreak Painter', about 500 BC.

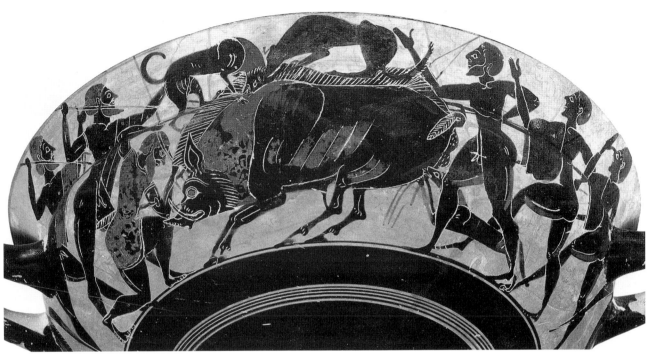

Men and dogs together have cornered the legendary Calydonian boar. Athenian cup, early 6th century BC.

was taken around piled high in baskets, a wine-waiter was always at hand. A singer sang stories of gods and heroes – stories just like the *Odyssey* itself, perhaps – and might earn a well-chosen cut of meat in reward for a well-told tale.

This was the scene that the mysterious beggar saw. Soon he was to throw off his disguise, to snatch down the bow that only he could draw, and to massacre the young men who had invaded his house, eaten up his livestock and slept with his slave-girls. Then at last he would taste once more the best wine from his dark storeroom, kept locked away by his old housekeeper to await his return.

There are no recipes in the *Iliad* or *Odyssey*. Yet the poet's vision of the world of the 'heroes' was so sharp and clear that we do hear a good deal of what he imagined they ate and drank. And his imagination ran to simple, hearty, roast meat. The dishes listed below are suggested in one way or another by the epics – and they serve to introduce all the main sources of recipes used in later chapters. Homer might well have been surprised by our selection of dishes, but he would not have been surprised by most of the individual ingredients or the flavours. We cannot suggest a Homeric sweet – except the fresh fruits of Alcinous' orchard, fruits that no one

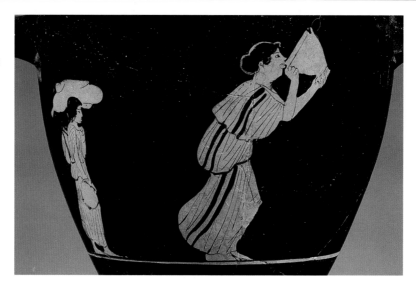

happens to bite into from beginning to end of the epic – but instead we have taken inspiration from Galen's description of a 'pancake', a dish whose history certainly does go back very nearly to the time of Homer.

Now to the wine that would accompany a Homeric feast. The priest Maron, who lived on the north Aegean coast of Greece, presented a fine gift to Odysseus in the course of his travels. Maron 'drew off for me sweet unmixed wine in twelve amphoras, a divine drink: none of the slaves or servants in his house had known it, but himself and his dear wife and one housekeeper only. And whenever he drank the honeyed red wine, filling a cup he poured it into twenty measures of water, and a marvellous sweet smell rose from the mixing bowl.' Some gullible Romans took every word of the epics as history. Pliny writes: 'Fame came earliest, we learn from Homer, to Maronean wine from the Aegean coast of Thrace. . . . Homer reported that Maronean was to be mixed with twenty parts of water. In that country the grape retains its strength and formidable power, for a very recent author, Mucianus (three times Consul), reported that when he was there he saw each pint being mixed with eight of water: it was black in colour, fragrant, and became fuller with age.'

We cannot really taste Maron's wine. We only know, from the phrases that came naturally to the poet, that Homeric wine was 'black' (as red wine really is, especially in earthenware cups), 'fiery', 'smoky' and sometimes 'sweet' or 'honeyed' – and that the host mixed it with water before it was served. For an epic feast, there can be no better choice of dry white wine than the firmly aromatic Mantinea, just such a wine as Menelaus' neighbours might have brought in for his sons' wedding feast

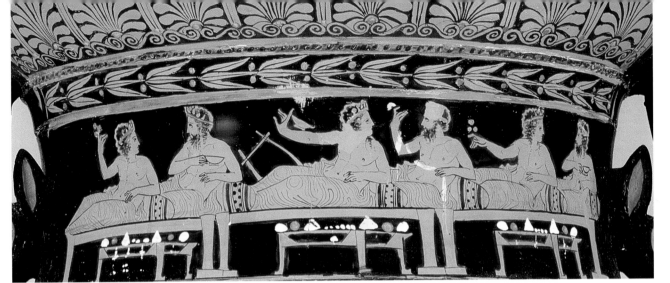

– or the lighter Robola of Cephallenia, where Odysseus is supposed to have held some land. Choose a powerful red wine: solid Nemea, perhaps, from the venerable vineyards in the hills north of Argos. Wine from here was surely good enough for Agamemnon. As a dessert white wine, there is the gloriously sweet and aromatic muscat of Lemnos, in the north Aegean, just off the Thracian coast. A Greek delicatessen can find all of these, and a Greek mineral water to go beside them. Whatever the heroes might think, we prefer to serve the water separately from the wine!

Feasting among the gods. There are cakes and fruits on the tables before each couch. Frieze from an Athenian wine-mixing bowl, probably by the 'Meleager Painter', about 390 BC.

Olive Relish

A maid poured water from a beautiful gold jug over the visitors' hands into a silver bowl, and drew up a carved table. An aged housekeeper had put out bread, adding many relishes, and encouraged them to taste all that was in the house. A waiter set out for them bronze trays of all sorts of meats, and gold drinking-cups. A servant often passed by to pour wine for them.
HOMER, *Odyssey* I, 136–43

How to make green, black or mixed olive relish. Remove stones from green, black or mixed olives, then prepare as follows: chop them and add oil, vinegar, coriander, cumin, fennel, rue, mint. Pot them: the oil should cover them. Ready to use.
CATO, *On Agriculture* 119

Cato is the early Roman soldier and politician whose farming handbook forms the basis of chapter 5. This recipe therefore dates from about

200 BC, but olives provided relish and flavouring all through ancient times. The olive tree had been under cultivation in Greece for a thousand years, if not longer, when the *Iliad* and *Odyssey* were composed; classical civilisation is almost unimaginable without it. At classical Greek banquets olives were served in brine, and sometimes, no doubt, they were served as relishes similar to this. Olive pastes and relishes are widely available today in delicatessens.

One or two details of the ancient recipe are unclear. By 'fennel, rue, mint' Cato seems to mean the fresh leaf of these herbs: so, I take it, with 'coriander', and I therefore assume that 'cumin' is also the green leaf. This is hard to find, and hard to grow, and I have therefore omitted it from the list of ingredients. Fennel leaf will also not be easy to find unless you grow it yourself, though that is not difficult: it must be fresh, as the leaf loses its flavour when dried. The distinctive aniseed flavour of fennel leaf is also found in the bulbous root of some modern varieties, which can now be found on sale as a vegetable, so the chopped root will serve as a substitute. To make life easier buy pitted olives – but do buy them loose, from an Italian or Greek delicatessen, not bottled, canned or vacuum-packed.

SERVES FOUR

4 OZ (120 G) BLACK OLIVES

4 OZ (120 G) GREEN OLIVES

4 TABLESPOONS (60 ML) RED WINE VINEGAR

4 TABLESPOONS (60 ML) OLIVE OIL

1 HEAPED TEASPOON CHOPPED FENNEL LEAF OR
FINELY DICED FENNEL ROOT

2 TEASPOONS CHOPPED FRESH CORIANDER

2 TEASPOONS DRIED OR CHOPPED FRESH RUE

2 HEAPED TEASPOONS DRIED OR 3 TEASPOONS CHOPPED FRESH MINT

Chop the olives roughly and pour on the vinegar and olive oil. Prepare the herbs, chopping them finely if fresh, and add to the mixture. Place the olive relish in a sealable container and pour a little olive oil over the top.

At this stage it can be eaten, as Cato firmly says, but I find that it improves with a few days' marinating. It is so delicious that I have rarely kept it for longer. Try it with pitta bread, accompanied by a sharp sheep's cheese such as feta.

Toronaean Shark or Tuna

In Torone you must buy belly steaks of the porbeagle shark. Sprinkling
them with cumin and a little salt you will add nothing else, my friend,
unless maybe green olive oil: when they are done you will be serving
chopped salad for dressing, and the steaks with it. As you cook all these
steaks, a 'crew' for your cooking pot, don't mix in a splash of water with
them, or wine vinegar, but just pour on oil by itself and dry cumin and
aromatic herbs. Cook over embers, not a fierce fire, and stir frequently to
take care that they do not burn.

ARCHESTRATUS 23

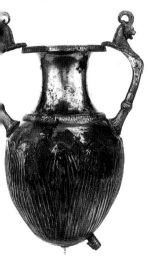

Wine-jar, silver with gilding, from the Persian Empire (soon to be conquered by Alexander). The handles are lion-griffins.

It amused later Greeks, who were enthusiasts for seafood, that Homer's heroes 'never ate a fish' – in spite of the fact that they spent ten years fighting at Troy, where plentiful tuna and many other fine fish were to be found. Meat was in reality a rare luxury for most Greeks, which is probably why the poet put so much emphasis on it. As archaeologists know, fish had already been part of the Greek diet for thousands of years, and no apology is needed for including it in an epic menu. Archestratus' instructions, quoted here, date from about 350 BC, but the method used in a household of Homer's time could well have been identical. Of the ingredients that Archestratus calls for, only cumin was not native to Greece. Even cumin is listed, among other aromatics, on the clay tablets in Linear B script used for keeping accounts in the Mycenaean palaces of the Bronze Age; so it reached Greece at least six hundred years before Homer.

Shark is rarely eaten in Britain except in restaurants – and that is a great pity. It is one of the meatiest of all the Mediterranean fishes, and surprisingly well-flavoured. In the USA the closely related mako has become deservedly more popular recently. If you can find only frozen (rather than chilled) shark, you may prefer to substitute tuna, which is more readily available chilled. If using frozen shark, ensure that it is thoroughly defrosted and drained: it can hold a great deal of water.

SERVES FOUR

4 SHARK OR TUNA STEAKS,
EACH WEIGHING ABOUT 4 OZ (120 G)

3 TABLESPOONS (45 ML) EXTRA-VIRGIN OLIVE OIL

2 TEASPOONS GROUND CUMIN

2 TEASPOONS CHOPPED FRESH OR DRIED MIXED HERBS
(PARSLEY, OREGANO, CORIANDER, MINT)

¼ TEASPOON SALT

Brush the steaks with olive oil. Combine the cumin, herbs and salt in one bowl. Press a little of this mixture on both sides of each steak and fry them in a little olive oil for 6 to 8 minutes on each side until they are golden-brown. Serve with a crisp green salad dressed with a tablespoon of olive oil, a tablespoon of red wine vinegar and a splash of fish sauce.

We shall see more of the trenchant opinions of the gourmet poet Archestratus in chapter 3. Here he insists, in his usual way, on the one Greek city that produced his chosen dish at its best. Torone was in ancient times the centre of a wine-exporting district on the central peninsula of three-pronged Chalcidice in northern Greece. No wine is exported from quiet Torone beach now, and not many visitors stop there, though the holiday resort of Porto Carras is just 15 miles up the coast.

Chicken Stuffed with Olives

*Bird: Put broken fresh olives in the cavity, sew up and boil.
Remove the olives when cooked.*
Apicius 6, 5, 7

SERVES TWO TO FOUR

6 OZ (170 G) BLACK OLIVES, PREFERABLY PITTED

1 SMALL FRESH CHICKEN

2 BAY LEAVES

SALT

10 BLACK PEPPERCORNS

1 ONION

1 CARROT

1 CELERY STALK

Chop the olives roughly and stuff the chicken with them. Using a large darning needle, sew up the cavity with cotton thread or fine cooking string. Place the chicken in a saucepan and cover with water. Add the bay leaf, salt, peppercorns and vegetables. Bring to the boil and simmer for 1½ hours until tender. Remove from the water and cool slightly before carving.

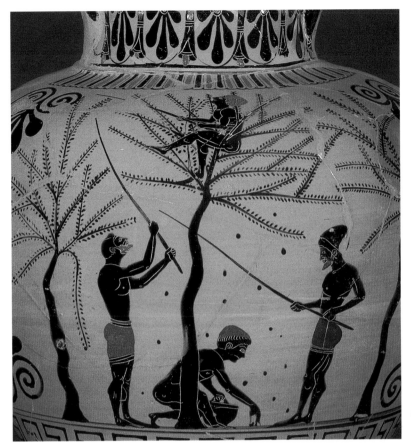

The olive harvest. Trees were said to fruit more steadily if not treated violently – but this was still the usual way. Athenian wine-jar of about 520 BC by the 'Antimenes Painter'.

Apicius is the well-known Roman cookery book of about AD 400 (see chapter 8). This is one of its simplest recipes, lacking the numerous spices of which so many *Apicius* recipes are full. It could have been prepared in almost any ancient household. The principle behind it is that the olives should give the chicken their flavour and then be discarded. This is fine in itself – but what a waste of olives! I therefore use pitted olives and serve them with the meat.

My inclination to experiment with ancient recipes beyond the confines of the text prompted me to try a number of variations on this dish. The peppercorns are my addition: they were available in Roman times, though not in early Greece. The chicken can be roasted instead of boiled, using olive oil with a little fish sauce as the medium. Olive relish (see page 31) can be used to form a stuffing if a small amount of cooked bulghur wheat is added to it – the result is excellent.

As for the chicken itself, by Homer's own time the first Greek cocks had probably crowed! The 'barnyard fowl', native to southern China, had gradually spread westwards to Greece: unmistakable vignettes of cocks and hens can be found in Greek vase-paintings of about 700 BC. They were exotic Eastern birds. Geese, however, were kept in Homeric farmyards, and were already being carefully fattened with wheat. Duck, goose, quail and pigeon would also be appropriate substitutes in this recipe.

Roast Kid or Lamb

'Set up a bigger bowl, son of Menoetius, and mix the wine stronger, and make a cup for each of them. These men that have come under my roof are very dear to me,' said Achilles; and Patroclus obeyed his good friend. Then he put down a big chopping-block in the light of the fire, and placed on it the back of a sheep and of a fat goat, and a hog's chine rich in lard. Automedon held the meat for him, and Achilles cut it up. He chopped it and stuck the pieces on skewers. Meanwhile godlike Patroclus made the fire into a great blaze, and then, when the fire had burnt out and the flames had died, he spread the embers and arranged the skewers above the fire, resting them on their supports, and he sprinkled the meat with holy salt. Then when he had roasted it and piled it on trays, Patroclus took bread and set it out on a table in fine baskets, and Achilles served the meat.
HOMER, *Iliad* 9, 202–17

Marinated kid or lamb: 1 pint milk, 4 oz honey, 1 oz pepper, a little salt, a little asafoetida. For the sauce: 2 fl oz oil, 2 fl oz fish sauce, 2 fl oz honey, 8 crushed dates, half pint good wine, a little starch.
Apicius 8, 6, 7

Roast kid or lamb will make a fine and appropriate centre to an epic feast. Lamb was the favourite meat for special occasions in ancient Greece, just as it is for a modern Easter. This recipe from *Apicius* is a first-class way to prepare roast lamb for a special dinner. It takes a little effort, but is well worth it. Discarding the marinade may seem wasteful, but it curdles when heated and would spoil the finished dish.

SERVES SIX

SHOULDER OF KID OR 2½ LB (1.25 KG) LEG OF LAMB

OLIVE OIL

Marinade

1 PINT (2½ CUPS/570 ML) MILK

4 OZ (½ CUP/120 G) CLEAR HONEY

1 TABLESPOON (30 G) PEPPER

SALT

½ TEASPOON ASAFOETIDA POWDER OR 5 DROPS ASAFOETIDA TINCTURE

Sauce

8 CRUSHED FRESH OR DRIED DATES

10 FL OZ (1¼ CUPS/280 ML) RED WINE

4 TABLESPOONS (60 ML) OLIVE OIL

2 TABLESPOONS (60 G) CLEAR HONEY

4 TABLESPOONS (60 ML) FISH SAUCE

A LITTLE CORNFLOUR (CORNSTARCH)

Combine the marinade ingredients and leave the meat overnight in the marinade, turning it occasionally to ensure full absorption. Soak the fresh or dried dates in a little red wine at the same time. The next day remove the meat from the marinade, pat it dry, and then roast it in an oven pre-heated to 400°F (200°C/gas mark 6), well seasoned and with olive oil. The timing should be 20 minutes to each 1 lb (450 g) and 20 minutes in addition. When the meat is nearly ready, pound the dates to a pulp and add to the remaining red wine, honey, fish sauce and oil. Bring to the boil and cook out briefly, and thicken with cornflour. When the joint is cooked, remove it from the oven and leave to rest for 10 minutes before carving thick slices and serving with a little of the sauce on the side.

This recipe is one of the few in the Roman cookery book that gives quantities. They seem accurate – at least, they work very well – and I have left them unaltered. The fact that quantities are given has suggested to some scholars that this was originally a Greek recipe. Perhaps more telling is that there are fewer herbs and spices in this dish than in other *Apicius* recipes. Even though it comes from a text a thousand years later than Homer – and even though pepper and asafoetida would have been unfamiliar to the epic poet – the recipe is not out of place in this chapter. It is particularly good with kid if you can find it. I managed to obtain some at a halal butcher in London. It will probably need to be ordered in advance, but repays the extra effort.

Pancakes with Honey and Sesame Seeds

Let us find time to speak of other cakes, the ones made with wheat flour. Teganitai, as we call them, are made simply with oil. The oil is put in a frying-pan resting on a smokeless fire, and when it has heated, the wheat flour, mixed with plenty of water, is poured on. Rapidly, as it fries in the oil, it sets and thickens like fresh cheese setting in the baskets. And at this point the cooks turn it, putting the visible side under, next to the pan, and bringing the sufficiently fried side, which was underneath at first, up on to the top, and when the underneath is set they turn it again another two or maybe three times till they think it is all equally cooked. Some mix it with honey, and others again with sea-salt.

GALEN, *On the Properties of Foods* I, 3

SERVES FOUR

4 OZ (I CUP/I20 G) FLOUR

8 FL OZ (I CUP/225 ML) WATER

2 TABLESPOONS (60 G) CLEAR HONEY

OIL FOR FRYING

I TABLESPOON (I5 G) TOASTED SESAME SEEDS

Mix the flour, water and 1 tablespoon honey together into a batter. Heat 2 tablespoons oil in a frying-pan and pour a quarter of the mixture into the fat. When it has set, turn it two or three times to give an even colour. Cook 3 more pancakes in the same way. Serve all 4 pancakes hot with the remainder of the honey poured over and sprinkled with sesame seeds.

It is a continual surprise how little food changes from one millennium to the next. The great physician Galen (AD I29–99), a tireless observer of details of food and drink, gives a description so serious and painstaking that we smile to imagine him making notes as he watched a cook turning pancakes. It is hard to remember that he is writing I800 years ago. What is more, the dish was already eight hundred years old in his time. The early Greek poet Hipponax had written of pancakes 'drugged with sesame seeds'. Comedy gluttons on the Athenian stage had spoken of 'mist rising at dewy daybreak from warm pancakes' and of honey poured over them as they sizzle: a breakfast meal, no doubt, and one that was possibly sold on the streets of ancient Athens from portable braziers.

OPPOSITE *The blind Phineus is tormented by winged harpies who befoul and steal his food. A scene from myth on an Athenian jug by the 'Cleophrades Painter', about 480 BC.*

You can serve modern pancakes with honey and toasted sesame seeds. However, what Galen is describing is not precisely the pancake familiar to us, but something as thick as a blini or even thicker, considering that it is to be turned so many times. I also suspect that more oil was used for frying than we would normally use, and this is reflected in the modern adaptation given above.

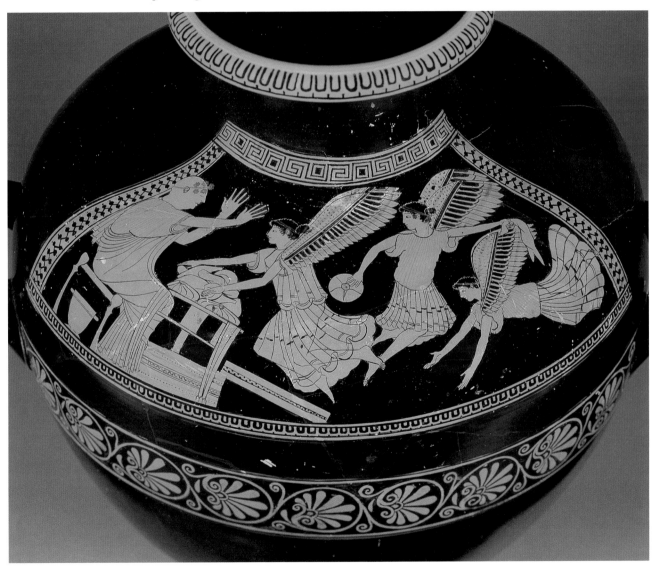

Porridge (Kykeon)

Fair-haired Hecamede made kykeon *for them – Hecamede whom the old man had got as his prize from Tenedos, selected for him by the Greeks because of his excellence as an adviser. First she moved a table up to them, a fine polished table with a dark gleaming stand: on it she placed a bronze dish with an onion in it as relish to the drink, and also yellow honey. Next came the heap of holy barley meal. Thus, in a cup, the lovely woman made a* kykeon *for them with Pramnian wine: she grated goat's cheese into it with a bronze grater, and sprinkled barley meal on it, and when she had prepared the* kykeon *she invited them to drink.*

HOMER, *Iliad* 11, 638–41

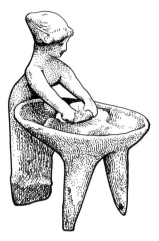

A woman grinds flour: Greek terracotta figurine.

What was this curious, nourishing brew that the captive woman prepared for Nestor's friends after a hard day's work at the siege of Troy? Whatever it was, it occurs again and again in early Greek poetry – and the reader soon comes to feel that it has a ritual element. As a mixture of wine and cereal, it brings together the gifts of Dionysus, the wine god, and of Demeter, the goddess who gave us wheat and barley. It could be made dangerously powerful, too. Women who knew about herbs could use a *kykeon* for strange purposes: perhaps to send men to sleep; perhaps worse. Circe 'stirred cheese and barley and yellow honey into Pramnian wine and mixed harmful drugs with this *kykeon*' to turn Odysseus' sailors into swine (see the drawing on page 28).

How, then, was *kykeon* made? It may be an impossible quest, but I have at least attempted to rediscover this food of the heroes. The first clue comes from the name itself, for *kykân* means to churn or clot or thicken by stirring. This suggests something like a soup or even a porridge. A Byzantine scholar made the very same connection: '*Kykeon* seems to have been somewhere between food and drink,' he argued. 'Perhaps really it was something that was supped like soup.'

At first I imagined that the thickening agent was the barley, and that it must stand in the wine until it becomes soft and chewy. But even then it does not truly clot or thicken. Was the barley ground before it was added? If so, it was roasted first, to remove it from its husks. The poet seems to specify 'roasted and ground meal', but even roasted and ground barley will not thicken the mixture. After various experiments I tried placing the wine, barley, honey and a little soft goat's cheese in a pan and heated the mixture. As would be expected, this made a very pleasant porridge.

A recipe in Cato's farming handbook confirmed that I might be getting near to the true nature of *kykeon*. 'Carthaginian porridge to be cooked thus,' he instructs. 'Put 1 lb emmer in water till it is thoroughly soaked.

Pour it into a clean vessel. To this add 3 lb new cheese, ½ lb honey, 1 egg. Mix all together well and turn into a new pot.' Emmer, a now rare species of wheat, would have been roasted while still in its husk and then ground by hand, probably to the texture of semolina. Substituting wine for Cato's water and eliminating the egg, which would thicken and enrich the mixture further, we have a very similar dish to *kykeon*.

Things become clearer. The soft new cheese – something like ricotta in texture – is the primary ingredient and the major thickening agent. The barley meal gives structure to the porridge and prevents curdling. The clotting and churning that define *kykeon*, however, are linked to the cheese, not the barley. When cooked out gently, this mixture produces a soft pourable porridge that could indeed be supped from the cup.

Cato's recipe is very good as it stands. Divide the quantities by four and use semolina instead of emmer.

SERVES FOUR

4 OZ (¾ CUP/120 G) SEMOLINA

12 OZ (375 G) RICOTTA CHEESE

2 TABLESPOONS (60 G) HONEY

A LITTLE BEATEN EGG

Place the semolina in just enough water to cover it and allow to soak for 10 to 15 minutes. When soft, drain away any remaining water and add the ricotta cheese, honey and beaten egg. Bring slowly to boiling point, but do not let it boil. Allow to simmer for a few minutes.

When all is said and done, these approaches to *kykeon* are, at best, informed guesses. The truth remains to be discovered: the pleasure in researching ancient cuisine is in the detective work, the hunt for clues that leads to unexpected tastes and textures and, with luck, may lead close to the original recipe.

In the mythical Garden of the Hesperides the golden apples are guarded by the snake Ladon, watched by Atlas' daughters. Heracles is soon to shoot the snake and retrieve three apples, his eleventh Labour.

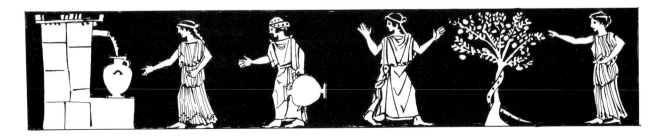

2

The Banquet
of Philoxenus

The usual picture of the parties and entertainments of classical
Athens seems to have room for little more than wine. The word
symposion meant, simply, 'drinking together'. Those rich enough
to have a house with more than one or two rooms would have a room set
aside for just this purpose, at least as formal as any English dining room.
It would be furnished with five or more couches around its walls, and its
size would be described in precisely this way – a 'five-couch room' or
whatever it might be. There would be small, easily portable tables to
stand in front of each couch.

There are more details in a unique document from Sicily or Greece of
around 400 BC, the strange sensuous *Banquet* of Philoxenus, a poetic
celebration of obsessive culinary pleasures, a literary dinner-party:

Water for our hands, a silver jug, a gentle child to pour it;
Goodly sprigs of slender myrtle woven for wreaths.
In came a pair of slaves with a shiny table, and another, and another, until
    they filled the room.
They fetched in snow-white barley-rolls in baskets,
A casserole – no, bigger than that – call it a *marmite*, full of a noble eel with
    a look of the conger about him,
Honey-glazed shrimps besides, my love,
Squid sprinkled with sea-salt,
Baby birds in flaky pastry,
And a baked tuna, gods! what a huge one, fresh from the fire and the pan
    and the carving-knife,
Enough steaks from its tender belly to delight us both as long as we might
    care to stay and munch.

Who was this unusual author? Modern editors assert that it was
Philoxenus of Leucas, a legendary glutton of whom it was said that he
practised drinking unbearably hot water and putting his hand into the hot
water flow at the baths, to train himself to snatch and swallow the best of
each dish as soon as it emerged from the oven.

But, glutton though he was, no one knows if Philoxenus of Leucas
wrote anything at all. It is more likely that the *Banquet* was written by the

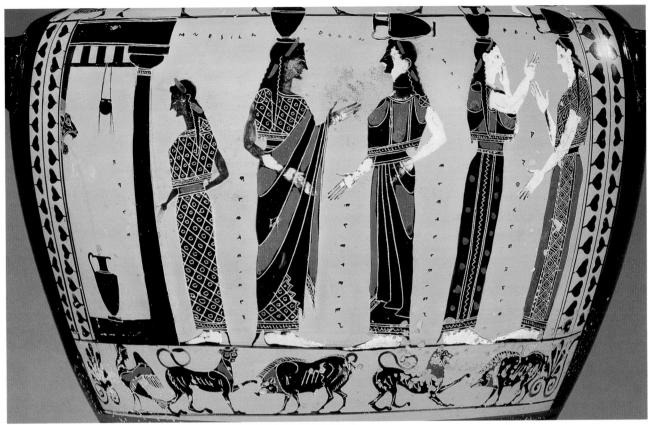

Women fetching water: their traditional opportunity to meet and talk.

once famous Philoxenus of Cythera, a much more interesting figure. He was court poet to the ruler of the Greek cities in Sicily, Dionysius I of Syracuse (*c.* 430–367 BC), and was best known for his tale *Galatea* in which the Cyclops falls in love with a mountain nymph. The unlucky Philoxenus, rumour said, had once been caught in bed with another Galatea, the king's mistress, and had been condemned to hard labour in the Syracusan quarries as a punishment. There is nothing of this, however, in the *Banquet*!

At last we had had our fill of food and drink:
The servants cleared away, and brought in warm water, soap and oil of
   orris to wash our hands.
They gave us muslin towels, divine perfumes, wreaths of violets.
Then the same polished tables, loaded up with more good things, sailed
   back to us, 'second tables' as men say:
Sweet pastry shells,

Crispy flapjacks,
Toasted sesame cakes drenched in honey sauce,
Cheesecake, made with milk and honey, a sweet that was baked like a pie;
Cheese-and-sesame sweetmeats fried in hottest oil and rolled in sesame
    seeds were passed around . . .

With the bringing in of clean tables came the break between dinner and drinking-party. At this stage, with the sweets and nuts, wine was first served; at this point in the evening, wherever they had eaten, leisured Greeks looked for a house where the wine promised to flow.

In a respectable house, the dining room was a place for men's dinners and drinking-parties. Women of the household would be out of sight, though dancers and flute-girls, hired for the occasion, might be seen in the dining room often enough.

Entertainment and wine; poetry and music; and often, it seems, deep and serious conversation. On the occasion that is described in Plato's famous *Symposium* – how realistically, no one knows – the philosopher Socrates (c. 470–399 BC), the satirical playwright Aristophanes and their companions debated the nature of love. The occasion for that famous conversation was simply this: their host, the poet Agathon, had invited his friends to celebrate his prize at the annual drama festival of Athens.

Two fat revellers:
'Dikaios Painter',
about 500 BC.

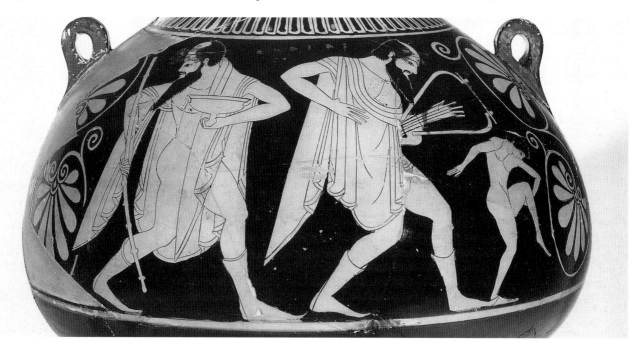

Socrates himself had been an unexpected arrival. Meeting in the street a friend who had been invited, the old philosopher was persuaded that Agathon would welcome an extra guest. Room was easily found on the couches, which were big enough for two guests and even, at a pinch, for three.

Did they want a flute-girl this time? She had been booked in advance, but the uninvited guest was in favour of conversation, not music. 'I think,' said Socrates, ' we should tell the flute-girl to go away and play to herself – or, if she fancies, to the women indoors.'

And so the discussion began. Aristophanes' fertile imagination told of the Creator who had taken beings that were originally spherical and sliced them into two. Some made two men, some made men and women, some made two women, and all of us are forever searching for our other halves. When Aristophanes' story was completed, each of the other participants gave his own ideas on the theme of love, its origin and its purpose.

The night advanced. A noise was heard in the yard, Plato tells us:

There was a knocking at the outer door, very noisy, as if it were a group of revellers: a flute-girl could be heard.

'Go and see, boys,' said Agathon. 'If it is anyone we like, invite them in. If not, say that we have finished drinking already.'

Symposium scene by Duris, about 430 BC. Cups and wine-jugs hang on the wall behind the drinkers, who are waited on by slave-boys.

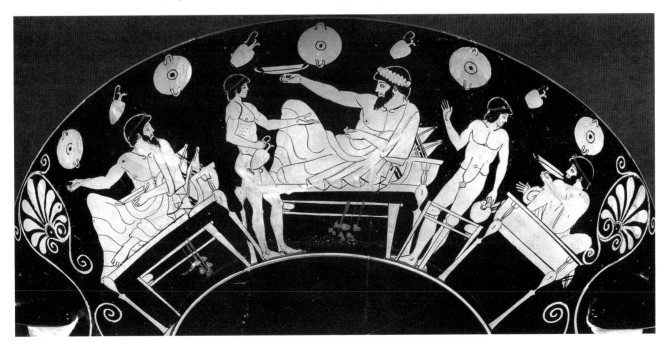

45

A little later they heard the voice of Alcibiades in the courtyard, very drunk and shouting out, 'Where's Agathon? Take me to Agathon!'

He was helped in by the flute-girl and some of his other cronies. He stood at the door crowned with a thick wreath of ivy and violets, with a great many ribbons dangling over his head, and said: 'Greetings, gentlemen. Will you take as fellow-drinker a man who is already very drunk indeed? Or shall we simply put a congratulatory garland on Agathon, our reason for coming, and go away?'

Alcibiades (*c.* 450–404 BC), once Socrates' pupil, now a flamboyant politician but later to be branded a traitor to Athens, was welcomed in. He was installed as the third occupant of Socrates' couch, and the discussion went on, sometimes bantering, sometimes serious. By daybreak the narrator concludes, most of the guests were asleep – but Socrates was still talking earnestly.

A more down-to-earth author, Xenophon, seems to have felt that Plato had given a false picture of the drinking-parties that Socrates attended. Xenophon's *Symposium* could hardly be more different. The conversation ranges at random over many subjects. There was entertainment, too, brought by an entrepreneur who went from door to door looking for parties. He owned a slave boy who danced and a girl who did acrobatics, leaping in and out of a ring of upturned swords. Socrates' contribution at Xenophon's drinking-party was not to send the entertainers away but to take charge of the programme. He felt that beauty could be displayed to better effect than among swords, and suggested an erotic dance that was performed by the two slaves together.

The recipes that follow will help to build a menu for a classical dinner-party. Several dishes are suggested by Philoxenus' lines just quoted, including the honey-glazed shrimps, the tuna steak and the barley rolls. A further short extract reminds us of some of the 'nibbles' that can be served as the wine continues to flow:

Fresh young chickpeas in safflower dip,
Eggs,
Young soft-skinned almonds,
Walnuts that children like to chew;
They served us all the things that are fit to serve at wealthy feasts.
The drinking, the games of *kottabos*, the clever talk, in which each smart
   new phrase in turn was greeted with applause,
All came to an end at last.

Athenians, in the fifth and fourth centuries, enjoyed wines from the Aegean coasts and especially those from the larger islands, Thasos, Lesbos, Chios. The philosopher and scientist Aristotle (*c.* 384–322 BC),

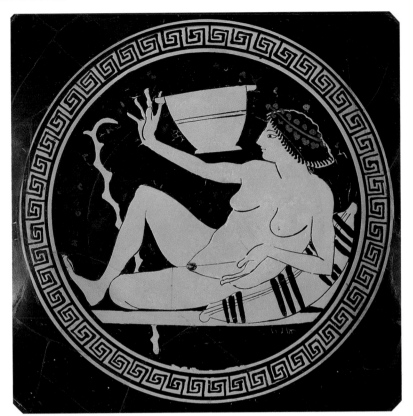

A party-girl shows her skill at kottabos: *the last drop of wine was propelled at a target with a clever flick of the wrist. Athenian cup, probably by Onesimus, about 500 BC.*

BELOW *Two women play* kottabos. *The one on the left says to her unseen lover: 'This one's for you, Euthymides.'*

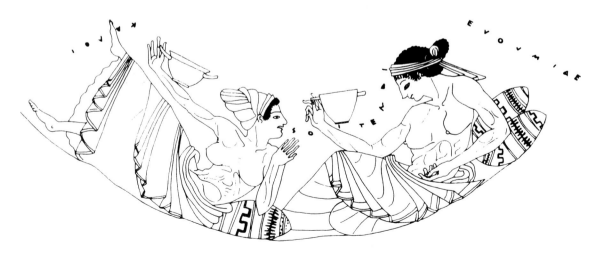

who lectured in Athens, was asked on his deathbed to name his successor. The choice lay between Eudemus of Rhodes and Theophrastus (*c.* 371–287 BC) of Eresus on Lesbos. The dying Aristotle sent for Rhodian wine. 'This is truly a sound and pleasant wine,' he said as he sipped it. Then he asked for a cup of Lesbian wine. 'Both are very good indeed,' he said, 'but the Lesbian is the sweeter.' His followers took the gentle hint and appointed Theophrastus to lead the school.

At least one later writer, the physician Galen, thought the wine of Theophrastus' home town Eresus to be the most aromatic and sweetest of all. The wines of these islands are not now often found outside Greece, but the heady muscat of Samos, well known since Byzantine times, will make a fine dessert wine and a stand-in for sweet Lesbian. For a modern representative of Chian, the island where 'black' wine was said to have been invented, we can look a little further afield. Chian vines were transplanted to Italy in Roman times. They could well be ancestors of the Aglianico ('Hellenic') grapes of some southern Italian vineyards. For a good smoky red with Greek ancestry, a fine accompaniment to game and roasts, therefore, choose Aglianico del Vulture.

Honey-glazed Shrimps

SERVES TWO

8 OZ (225 G) COOKED, PEELED SHRIMPS

I TABLESPOON (15 ML) OLIVE OIL

2 TABLESPOONS (30 ML) FISH SAUCE

I TABLESPOON (30 G) CLEAR HONEY

2 TEASPOONS CHOPPED FRESH OREGANO

BLACK PEPPER

If using frozen shrimps, ensure that they are well defrosted and drained. Place the oil, fish sauce and honey in a saucepan and add the shrimps. Sauté them gently in the cooking liquor for 2 or 3 minutes until they are tender. Remove them with a perforated spoon and keep warm. Continue to cook out the liquor until it has reduced by half. Add the chopped oregano and pour the sauce over the shrimps. Sprinkle with freshly ground black pepper. Serve as a first course with a crusty loaf and a simple salad.

This recipe is adapted from various ancient sources: Philoxenus makes the shrimps sound tasty, but his poem does not help in recreating the dish! Fish sauce (for its salt) and olive oil would undoubtedly have been among the ingredients, along with the honey. Oregano is suggested because the Greeks were well aware of its suitability in seafood dishes.

Tuna Steak

This young salted tuna first: it cost two obols. It has to be rinsed very well. Then, seasoning a small casserole, placing the slice in it, pouring white wine over, adding a coating of oil, and then simmering, I shall make it as good as marrow, finally tinselling it generously with silphium.
Alexis 186, quoted in ATHENAEUS 117d

SERVES TWO

2 TUNA STEAKS

WHITE WINE TO COVER

SALT AND PEPPER

2 TABLESPOONS (30 ML) OLIVE OIL

3 DROPS ASAFOETIDA TINCTURE

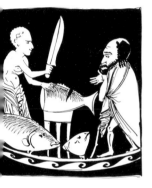

A shopper haggles with a fishmonger over tuna steaks.

Use a medium white wine and barely cover the steaks: season with salt and pepper and add the olive oil. The steaks can be cooked on top of the stove or in the oven and should be ready in about 20 to 25 minutes, depending on their thickness. Before serving add the asafoetida tincture to the liquor and reduce a little.

The original recipe (a snippet from an Athenian comedy) is for *Tarikhos horaion*, which seems to be one-year-old tuna caught 'in season' – that is, on its journey from the Black Sea to the Mediterranean – and then salted, which explains why the cook insists on the fact that the steak should be rinsed to remove unwanted saltiness. This delightful recipe is typical of the Greek preference for preparing food simply and without fuss.

'If you should come to the holy city of Byzantium,' wrote the gourmet Archestratus, 'eat another slice of *horaion* for me there: it is good and tender.' The tuna of Istanbul is, indeed, unbeatable. Nowadays we can buy frozen tuna steaks with little trouble, but it can also be found fresh-chilled at good fishmongers and some supermarkets and is well worth the search.

Cabbage the Athenian Way

*Cabbage should be sliced with the sharpest possible iron blade, then
washed, drained, and chopped with plenty of coriander and rue. Then
sprinkle with honey vinegar and add just a little bit of silphium.
Incidentally, you can eat this as a* meze.
Mnesitheus, quoted in ORIBASIUS, *Medical Collections* 4, 4, 1

Oxymeli *[honey vinegar]: Simmer honey till it foams, discard the scum,
add enough vinegar to make it neither too sharp nor too sweet, boil again
till it is mixed and not raw. For use, mix with water, just as you would
mix wine with water.*
GALEN, *Staying Healthy* 4, 6

SERVES SIX

1 SMALL WHITE CABBAGE

2 HEAPED TEASPOONS CHOPPED FRESH GREEN CORIANDER IN OIL

2 TEASPOONS CHOPPED FRESH OR DRIED RUE

2 PINCHES ASAFOETIDA POWDER

SALT

Honey Vinegar

4 OZ (½ CUP/120 G) HONEY

2 TABLESPOONS (30 ML) RED WINE VINEGAR

First make the honey vinegar. Follow Galen's advice: boil the honey and
skim it, add the vinegar and reduce a little. Store until needed.

Finely slice the cabbage; wash and drain it. Toss with the herbs and
3 tablespoons honey vinegar and sprinkle with the asafoetida powder and
a little salt.

This is quite a popular recipe among Greek and Roman writers.
Oribasius (fourth century AD), a well-known doctor of the late Roman
Empire, has borrowed it from a much older book of dietary advice by
Mnesitheus (fourth century BC), a medical writer from Athens. The
doctors are interested in this dish because it cured headaches and was
good for stomach upsets. At least, that is the claim made by the
encyclopaedist Pliny: he gives another version of the recipe, one that he
had found in Cato's farming handbook (where it was recommended for

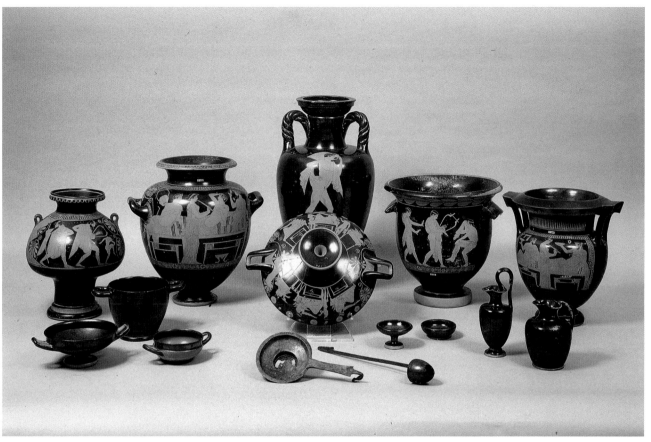

stiff joints). It is from the recipe of Cato (*c.* 234–149 BC) that I have borrowed the salt in my modern version.

Whatever its medicinal value, Mnesitheus was quite right about cabbage in honey vinegar being delicious as a starter or side dish. It still is, and is simple to prepare.

Romans were enthusiastic growers and eaters of cabbage. Pliny describes three types. The first was a curly one whose leaves were 'like parsley', comparable perhaps to Savoy cabbage. The second had broad leaves that could be seen growing from the stem, like kale or spring cabbage. The third had tight, closely packed leaves and appears to have been a white cabbage. He goes on to outline how many illnesses cabbage could cure. It was used as a poultice for wounds. If taken before a meal it prevented drunkenness, and if taken after drinking it could cure a hangover, but sadly our experience doesn't confirm this!

Equipment for wine. Back, left to right: a psykter *(wine-cooler); a* stamnos *and an* amphora *(storage jars), the latter showing a young man carrying an amphora on his shoulder; two* kraters *(mixing bowls). Centre: wine-ladle and strainer in front of a* kylix *(cup), upturned. Left and right foreground: cups, jugs and two small dishes for nuts or sweets.*

Barley Rolls

First I shall recall the gifts to humankind of fair-haired Demeter, friend
Moschus: take them to your heart. The best one can get, the finest of all,
cleanly hulled from good ripe ears, is the barley from the sea-washed breast
of famous Eresus in Lesbos – whiter than airborne snow. If the gods eat
barley, this is where Hermes goes shopping for it.
ARCHESTRATUS 4

Among the cereals, barley was the most popular in ancient Greece, as
Archestratus' enthusiasm attests, but even there it was not all that often
used for bread. In Rome, by contrast, barley was the punishment ration
for soldiers. Under the Roman Empire, Greeks too came to despise the
grain that grows so well in the Greek climate.

Barley is very low in gluten. When only pure barley meal is used for
bread, the resulting loaf is flat and heavy. Its keeping qualities are poor;
the crust and texture can be very dry. It seems likely that ancient bakers,
if preparing barley rolls for an elaborate banquet such as Philoxenus
describes, would have mixed their barley meal with some other flour to
produce a lighter loaf: coarse bread would be out of place. Elizabeth
David, in her definitive *English Bread and Yeast Cookery*, recommends a
50 per cent mixture of barley meal and strong wholewheat flour, which I
have followed. She also quotes a very simple barley bread recipe,
originating in Cornwall, that is remarkably well adapted to classical tastes
and kitchens and which provides the basis for the recipe given above:
'Cover the newly mixed bread with a cloth and set in a warm place. When
risen form into cone-shaped loaves and bake under a kettle on the hearth.
The loaves were usually grouped in threes, and the soft crust, where the
loaves touched each other, was called kissing crusts.'

Greeks and Romans too baked on the hearth under a brick, or *testum*.
The fact that the rolls will be touching under such a cover will ensure a
moist and soft crust. Cooks piled red-hot coals over the *testum*, creating a
mini-oven on the open hearth. This we cannot really duplicate: all that we
can do is to heat the container that we use. The brick can be replaced by a
large casserole or any large metal or crockery bowl that is ovenproof.
Many of the *testa* found by archaeologists have a small number of holes
in the top. I have experimented with a large, shallow, clay flowerpot,
12 in (30 cm) across and about 5 in (13 cm) deep. The drainage holes in
the top of this allow air circulation. If your own 'baking brick' does not
provide air holes, prop one side of the container about 1 in (2.5 cm) above
the baking tray. You may have to bake twice if your container is too small
to cover all the rolls.

MAKES TWELVE

Leaven

2 OZ (½ CUP/60 G) BARLEY FLOUR

1 TEASPOON FRESH OR ½ TEASPOON DRIED YEAST

Dough

6 OZ (1½ CUPS/170 G) STRONG WHOLEWHEAT FLOUR

6 OZ (1½ CUPS/170 G) BARLEY FLOUR

1 TEASPOON SALT

For the leaven, dissolve the yeast in 1 tablespoon (15 ml) warm water and use to form a dough with 2 oz (½ cup/60 g) barley flour. Knead the dough briefly, mould into a pat, cross it lightly and put a thumb-print in the centre. Pour 2 teaspoons of warm water into the indentation. Place in a glass dish with a lid and leave to ferment in a warm place for at least 24 hours.

Now for the dough: sift the wholewheat and barley flours together, add 1 teaspoon salt and the leaven and form a dough with sufficient warm water. Knead well and allow to rest and rise in a bowl, covered with plastic wrap or a plastic bag, in a warm place until it has doubled in size. Divide the dough into 12 pieces and mould them with the palm of your hand into smooth balls. Leave to rise in a warm place, covered with a cloth.

Heat the oven to 400°F (200°C/gas mark 6) and also heat a baking tray and an upturned casserole, shallow clay pot or metal bowl – whatever you decide to use as a 'baking brick'. Brush the tray with a little olive oil and place the rolls in 2 circles of 6, with the edges barely touching. Cover with the upturned container and bake for 15 to 20 minutes until lightly golden and hollow-sounding when tapped.

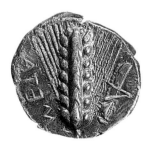

Food and drink often suggested coin designs. Metapontum (southern Italy), ear of wheat and locust.

Cheese and Sesame Sweetmeats

Globi to be made thus: mix cheese and semolina as above; make as many balls as you want. Put fat in a hot copper pan: fry one or two at a time, turning them frequently with a pair of spatulas. When cooked, remove them, coat in honey, sprinkle with poppy-seeds, serve.

CATO, *On Agriculture* 79

The cheese and sesame sweetmeats of Philoxenus were such a tempting idea that I resolved to work out a recipe that would reflect something of the ancient flavour. A recipe in Cato's farming manual forms the basis, yet his recipe is anything but complete. 'As above' seems to send the reader back to Cato's recipe for Layered Cheesecake (see page 94); in that recipe, however, the cheese and semolina are separate components.

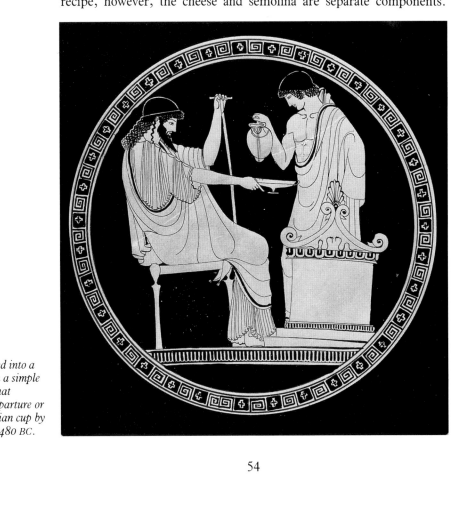

Wine is poured into a kylix (cup) in a simple ritual scene that symbolises departure or death. Athenian cup by Duris, about 480 BC.

Some enlightened guesswork is needed to fill the gaps in the Roman instructions. What follows, then, is one way to recreate the cheese and sesame sweetmeats of Philoxenus and Cato. I prefer to use not lard but olive oil as a deep-frying medium – it was certainly more popular among the Greeks and Romans themselves.

MAKES ABOUT FIFTEEN

10 FL OZ (1¼ CUPS/280 ML) MILK

2 OZ (2 TABLESPOONS/60 G) SEMOLINA

3 TABLESPOONS (90 G) HONEY

4 OZ (120 G) RICOTTA CHEESE

3 OZ (¾ CUP/85 G) SESAME SEEDS, LIGHTLY ROASTED

OLIVE OR VEGETABLE OIL FOR DEEP-FRYING

Bring the milk to the boil and sprinkle the semolina over it, stirring all the time. Cook out briefly, taking care not to let it burn. Turn into a clean bowl and allow to cool slightly, stirring occasionally. This should give a firm paste. When it is cooler, add 1 tablespoon honey and the ricotta. Mix well and stir in 2 oz (2 tablespoons/60 g) roasted sesame seeds.

Prepare a simple deep-fryer in a saucepan using olive or vegetable oil. Test the oil for temperature by dropping a little of the mixture in the oil: when it rises and begins to colour, the oil is ready. Form quenelles using 2 teaspoons: take a small amount of mixture in one spoon, cup the other spoon around it and pull it off; repeat the action until you have a smooth egg-shaped ball. Drop 2 or 3 sweetmeats at a time into the hot fat and turn them occasionally until they are golden-brown. Lift from the oil and drain on paper towels. Cook the rest of the sweetmeats in the same way. Warm the remaining honey and toss the cooked sweetmeats in it, then toss in the remaining roasted sesame seeds. These sweetmeats are delicious eaten either hot or cold.

3

THE MARKETS OF
THE MEDITERRANEAN

The Mediterranean world in which the Greek cities flourished –
and fought one another – was at least as open to travel and trade as
it is now. It was a world of ominous political changes. In that,
also, it resembles the present day.

The Greeks had founded cities in much of Sicily, in southern Italy and
along the Mediterranean coasts of what is now France and Spain. The
African coast, however, had been colonised by Phoenicians from Syria.
Their new metropolis, Carthage, dominated the southern seaways and
continually disputed possession of Sicily with the Greek monarchs of
Syracuse. Phoenicia itself now provided a Mediterranean fleet for the
great Persian Empire, which had threatened to conquer Greece and was
often involved behind the scenes in petty wars between Greek cities.
Meanwhile, on the northern shores of the Aegean, the power of the kings
of Macedon, the wily Perdiccas (died 413 BC) and his successors, was
growing.

It took five months to sail from southern Spain to the eastern end of the
Black Sea. Five months was almost a whole sailing season, for long-
distance voyages in winter were avoided. Shipwrecks were enough of a
risk even in summer.

These long sea routes were busy with merchantmen, with fishing
boats, and often with pirate vessels and warships. Trade was a risky and
complicated business: almost every city had its own currency, its own
laws and market regulations, its shortages and surpluses. Even so, there
were many who invested in trade, and some who became rich. A city such
as Athens had grown prosperous on the trade of the Aegean and the
Mediterranean, in spite of Spartan rivalry, in spite of Macedonian and
Thracian threats. In a scrap of Athenian comedy we can read a kind of
hymn, satirical yet truthful, to the wealth that came to Athens by sea:

Tell me now, Muses, how many good things the god Dionysus brings us in
his black ship as he plies the wine-dark sea. From Cyrene, silphium and
oxhide; from the Hellespont, mackerel and every salt fish; from Thessaly,
porridge and ox ribs; from King Sitalces, an itch for the Spartans; from King

56

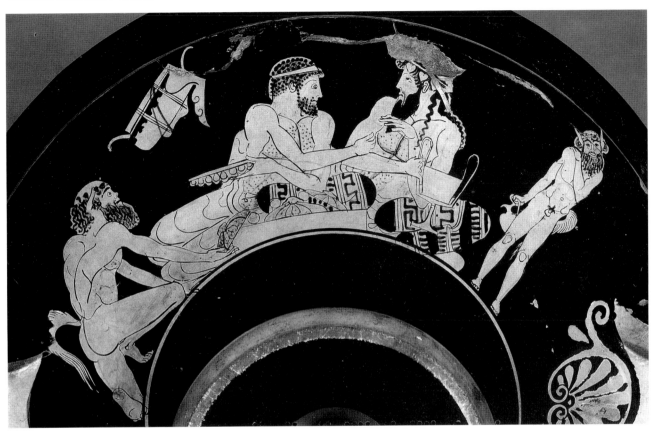

Perdiccas, many a shipload of lies. The Syracusans send us pigs and cheese; as for the people of Corfu, may the sea-god Poseidon damn them in their slick ships, for they have shifty thoughts! Incense from Syria; fair Crete provides cypress-wood for sacrifices; Africa has ivory for sale; Rhodes has dreamy raisins and figs. From Euboea come pears and fat apples; slaves from Phrygia; mercenaries from Arcadia. The Paphlagonians send us the chestnuts and glossy almonds which are the ornaments of any feast. Phoenicia provides wheat and the fruit of the date-palm; Carthage sends rugs and fancy pillows.

Trading laws and regulations were often inscribed on stone to be appealed to by either side in a dispute. On one of these inscriptions we can read that the citizens of the prosperous island of Thasos tried to control local trade in wine: 'Must nor wine, the fruit on the vine shall not be bought before the New Moon of Plynteria: any offending buyer shall pay a fine, stater for stater. . . . No Thasian ship shall land foreign wine

A slight dispute among the gods? Heracles feasts with Dionysus, attended by satyrs.

between Mount Athos and Cape Pacheia, or it shall pay the same penalty as for serving water for wine, and the pilot shall pay the same . . .'

There was trade in many other commodities besides food and wine. Athens reached a wide market with the fine painted pottery that provides some of the illustrations in this book. Slaves, including people who were kidnapped by pirates or captured in war, were bought and sold. Other people travelled voluntarily to find a living – including cooks, for Syrian bakers and Sicilian cooks were already widely sought after.

However, food was certainly the centre of interest at many harbour markets of the ancient Mediterranean. In one comedy after another, on the Athenian stage, hosts and cooks boasted of the fish they had found at market. We know something more of the quality and variety of market produce in those times thanks to a most unusual writer of about 350 BC.

Archestratus was a Sicilian who 'circumnavigated the world to satisfy his hunger – and even lower appetites', said a Roman scholar: quite unfairly, because to judge by his surviving poetry Archestratus wrote only about food! He must certainly have been an inveterate traveller. How else could he have found out about the specialities of all these small seaside cities, well over fifty of them, from Sicily to the Black Sea? Most

BELOW AND OPPOSITE Kylix (cup) by a painter working for Brygos. The entertainment is perhaps at a courtesan's establishment: boots and walking-sticks suggest that the men are guests.

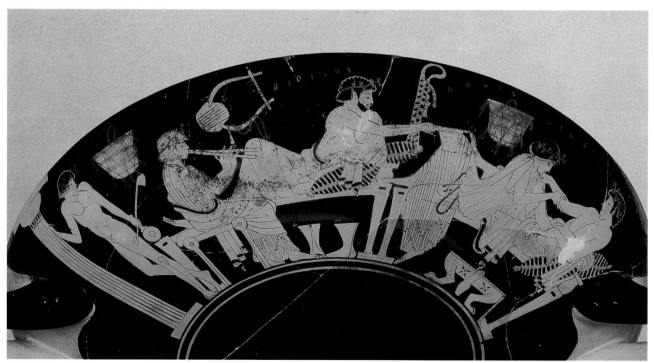

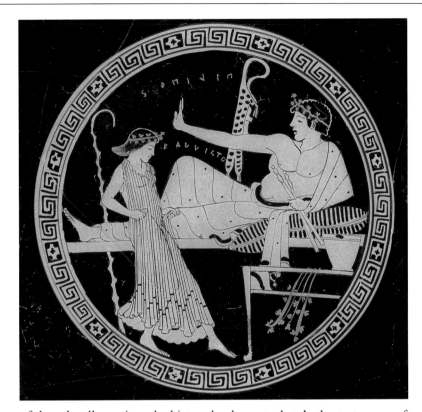

of them hardly get into the history books; yet what Archestratus says of them rings true, and their specialities are sometimes exactly the same now as they were 2400 years ago.

Archestratus had no time for fancy dinner-parties or complicated food: 'All to dine at one hospitable table,' he wrote; 'there shall be three or four friends altogether or at most five, or you would have a tentful of plundering mercenaries.' In writing of food his chief concern, repeated over and over again in different words, was that the true flavour of fresh produce, chosen in the right place at the right time of year, should be allowed to come through and not be covered up with layers of spices and strong seasonings. We gave one recipe from Archestratus in chapter 1, and in chapter 2 we quoted him on the barley of Lesbos. Here, now, is a typical recipe of his:

In autumn, as the Pleiades go down, you can cook bonito – and you can cook it in any way you please. Why should I spell the methods out for you? You could not spoil it if you tried. But if you want to be told this too, friend Moschus: the very best way for you to deal with this fish is to use fig leaves and fresh oregano (not very much), no cheese, no nonsense. Just wrap it up nicely in fig leaves fastened above with string, then hide it under hot ashes, keeping a watch on the time when it will be baked. Don't overcook it. Get it from beautiful Byzantium, if you want it to be good: and if you have it from somewhere near there, it will be respectable. The further from the Dardanelles, the worse it will be!

Archestratus was ready, too, to advise on the choice of bread to eat alongside his recipes: 'Take a Thessalian roll, a circling whirl of dough well kneaded under hand. They call it "crumble" in Thessaly; emmer bread is what others say. I also commend a child of durum wheat, the bread of Tegea that is baked under ashes. Fair is the loaf that famous Athens sells to mortals in her market-place; those from the clay ovens of vinous Erythrae, white and blooming with the gentle seasons, are a joy with dinner.'

What to drink with the Mediterranean menu set out in this chapter? Archestratus' answer to the question would certainly be: if you have no stores of old wine, drink the best wine available for tasting on the market on the day of your meal. Even in those days, there were too many wines for anyone to be able to judge fairly among all of them. The philosopher Democritus (fifth century BC) alone believed that it was possible to count grape varieties. 'He claimed to know every variety to be found in Greece. Others have pronounced them uncountable and infinite,' said Pliny.

Archestratus himself (like Aristotle!) preferred the taste of Lesbian wine, but he also praised the aroma of the Phoenician wine that came from Byblos. This was not too different, perhaps, from the 'wine of Helbon' that Persian emperors drank and that the prophet Ezekiel saw exported from Tyre. As a modern stand-in for the red wine that Archestratus might have drunk we can take the remarkable Château Musar of Lebanon. Otherwise, for this chapter, it is appropriate to look to Sicily and to suggest wines from what was not only a very early site of Greek colonisation but also one of the earliest homes of Greek gastronomy. There is the heavy red Corvo, the widely marketed table wine of Archestratus' native island. Fish dishes, however, usually call for white wine. Here Sicily can offer white Corvo – or you might find a lighter Sicilian white made from the Grecanico grape that, from its name, ought to have something Greek in its ancestry. Fine sweet whites, apart from the well-known Marsala (an eighteenth-century invention), come from the small islands off Sicily. Moscato di Pantelleria and Malvasia delle Lipari both bear names that link them with Byzantine Greece. Muscat was the favourite of many a medieval traveller to Constantinople. Malvasia, or Malmsey as the variety is known in English, is named after the trading port of Monemvasia.

Bream in Cheese and Oil

Bake bream at seaside Carthage: first rinse it well. You will see a good big one at Byzantium too, with a body the size of a round shield. Deal with it whole, thus: when you have taken it and coated it well all over with cheese and oil, hang it up in a hot clay oven and then bake it through. Sprinkle with cumin-rubbed salt and grey-green oil, drenching it generously with the divine liquid.

ARCHESTRATUS 13

SERVES FOUR

1 SEA BREAM OR PORGY, WEIGHING ABOUT 3 LB (1.5 KG)

8 OZ (225 G) PECORINO ROMANO CHEESE

3 TABLESPOONS (45 ML) OLIVE OIL

1 TEASPOON SALT

1 TEASPOON GROUND CUMIN

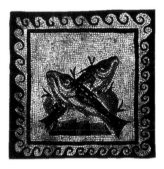

This and other similar vignettes later in this book are from a Roman mosaic from Toragnola in Italy.

Clean and carefully descale the fish, remove the fins and take off the head. Break up the cheese and put it in a food processor with the oil. (It can be pounded in a mortar if you have no food processor.) Process for a few minutes until you have a smooth, firm paste. Brush a non-stick baking tray with olive oil or line it with baking parchment and lay the fish on this. Spread half the cheese mixture over the fish, ensuring that the skin is completely hidden by the cheese. Carefully turn over the fish and repeat. Heat the oven to 425°F (220°C/gas mark 7) and bake the fish for 10 minutes. Take it out of the oven, carefully turn it over and return for a further 10 to 15 minutes. Mix the salt and cumin together and sprinkle it over the crust. Finish with a tablespoon of olive oil dribbled over the fish.

This is a delicious combination of tastes. The pungent sheep's cheese and delicate flavour of the fish meld very well. However, there are practical difficulties in duplicating Archestratus' method. It proves impossible to generate the fierce temperatures of a clay oven in a domestic setting, and without this heat the dish cannot be precisely recreated. Under the fiercest temperatures possible in a modern oven the cheese melts and falls off – and makes an awful mess of the oven! After experiments with various cheeses I settled on Pecorino Romano, which is similar to Parmesan in texture and is the most stable under intense heat. The method that Archestratus recommends, if we could follow it, would allow the cheese to 'set' as a crust around the fish, sealing in the juices. I have attempted to recreate this texture while baking the fish conventionally.

Archestratus specifies *sparos*, annular bream, a species that tends to be on the small side. Greeks and Romans knew well over a dozen different kinds of bream, many of them corresponding better with what the recipe seems to say about the size of the fish. Evidently larger bream could be substituted, but they are difficult to obtain and the smaller are actually ideal for this adaptation.

In North America, the bream family (*Sparidae*) is represented by the porgy. Choose a small variety to recreate this recipe.

Rock Eel with Mulberry Sauce

*A big rock eel was to hand: I baked the middle cuts, and I'll poach what's
left over and make a mulberry sauce.*
Sotades Comicus, quoted by ATHENAEUS 293a-d

SERVES FOUR

8 OZ (225 G) BLACKBERRIES (OR MULBERRIES IF AVAILABLE)

5 FL OZ (⅔ CUP/150 ML) RED WINE

4 ROCK EEL STEAKS

5 FL OZ (⅔ CUP/150 ML) WHITE WINE

BOUQUET GARNI OF OREGANO AND RUE

2 TABLESPOONS (60 G) HONEY

2 TABLESPOONS (30 ML) FISH SAUCE

I TABLESPOON (15 ML) VINEGAR

3 DROPS ASAFOETIDA TINCTURE OR ½ TEASPOON ASAFOETIDA POWDER

A LITTLE CORNFLOUR (CORNSTARCH)

Wash and pick over the fruit and place it with the red wine in a saucepan to heat. Poach the fish steaks in the white wine with the bouquet garni. Remove the fish and keep warm. Add the white wine and the bouquet to the fruit and cook out for 10 to 15 minutes. Add the honey, fish sauce, vinegar and asafoetida. Pass the sauce through a strainer: push the pulp through, leaving the seeds. Return to the heat and thicken with a little cornflour. Serve the fish steaks with a little sauce poured over one edge.

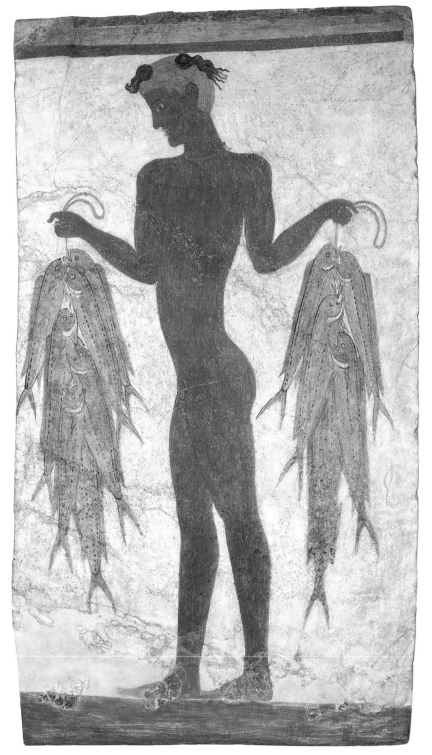

Fisherman with a catch of dolphin-fish (Coryphaena hippurus): wall-painting from Akrotiri, the town destroyed by the eruption of Thera, Santorini, in about 1530–1500 BC.

The fish referred to here have many names: smoothhound and rough hound, huss, dogfish, rock salmon, rock eel. Under one name or another they are readily available from fishmongers. They are not really eels or salmon but relatives of the shark, though smaller and not so dangerous! Some do grow to around 5 ft (1.5 m) long: their prey is crabs and lobsters. The flesh is pink, firm and delicately flavoured. In Britain rock eel is a fish-and-chip-shop fish, usually eaten in batter, though it deserves better.

Obedient to the comedy cook's instruction to make a mulberry sauce I have developed a recipe that combines elements of the sauces prescribed for fish in both Greek and Roman texts. Mulberries are a tree fruit similar in appearance to blackberries. They have a very short season and, unless you have a mulberry tree, are hard to find. I use blackberries: they serve well unless you are lucky enough to obtain the real thing.

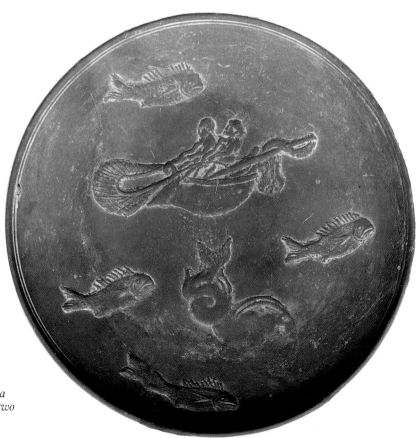

Platter from Roman North Africa, 3rd century AD. A sea scene: in the centre, two fishermen struggle to pull in their net.

Fish in Coriander Crust

Prepare the fish carefully, put in a mortar salt and coriander seed, crush finely, roll the fish in it, put in a baking dish, cover, seal, bake in the bread-oven. When cooked remove, season with very sharp vinegar and serve.

Apicius 10, 1, 4

SERVES TWO

2 TABLESPOONS (30 G) CORIANDER SEEDS

I TEASPOON SALT

2 FILLETS OF COD, HADDOCK OR PLAICE

WHITE WINE VINEGAR

Roast the coriander seeds in a baking dish in a pre-heated oven at 375°F (190°C/gas mark 5) for 10 minutes. Cool slightly, then pound with the salt in a mortar until you have a well-broken mixture. Pat the fish fillets dry with kitchen paper and feel along the back for and remove any small bones. Roll the fillets in the mixture as if it were breadcrumbs, then place them in an oiled casserole and cover with a lid. Place in the oven and cook for 20 to 25 minutes. Serve immediately, sprinkled with a good white wine vinegar.

This ancient equivalent of fish in breadcrumbs is remarkably good, and the method is suitable for many kinds of white fish. Don't forget (as I once did) to sprinkle it with vinegar before serving: it is dry and unpalatable without this final touch.

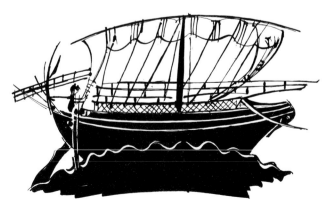

Merchant ship from an Athenian cup of about 500 BC.

Salt Meat Stew

Salt meat or slices of gammon (fresh meat similarly). Salt meats are first boiled by themselves to remove saltiness. Then all goes into a casserole: four parts wine, two parts must, one part vinegar, coriander seed, thyme, anise, fennel all roasted and put in at the beginning. Simmer. When half done, add honey and a bit of cumin (some also add pepper), and, putting the stew into a warm serving-vessel, add bits of warm bread.
Oxyrhynchus cookery book (see also p. 76)

Serves Four

I LB (450 G) GAMMON JOINT OR SMOKED HAM

I PINT (2½ CUPS/570 ML) WHITE WINE

10 FL OZ (1¼ CUPS/280 ML) WHITE GRAPE JUICE

5 FL OZ (⅔ CUP/150 ML) WHITE WINE VINEGAR

2 TEASPOONS CORIANDER SEEDS

I TEASPOON ANISEED

I TEASPOON FENNEL SEEDS

6 SMALL SPRIGS OF THYME

I TEASPOON GROUND CUMIN

I TABLESPOON (30 G) HONEY

½ TEASPOON COARSELY GROUND BLACK PEPPER

2 THICK SLICES COARSE WHOLEWHEAT BREAD

Cut the meat into small chunks, cover with water in a pan and bring to the boil. Discard the water, pour the wine, grape juice and vinegar over the meat and return to the heat. Combine the whole spice seeds and the thyme, spread on a baking tray and dry-roast them for 10 minutes in the oven at 400°F (200°C/gas mark 6). Shred the leaves from the stems of the thyme and place them in a mortar along with the seeds. Pound them until they are like breadcrumbs. Add this mixture to the stew and continue to simmer. Cook the stew for a total of 45 minutes. Towards the end add the cumin, honey and pepper. Cut the bread into chunks and place them in the oven for 5 minutes to dry them out a little. Add the bread to the stew: it will eventually soak up and thicken the juices.

This is a simple yet appetising stew, a peasant meal with the addition of more spices than would be available to most peasants. It is recorded in a

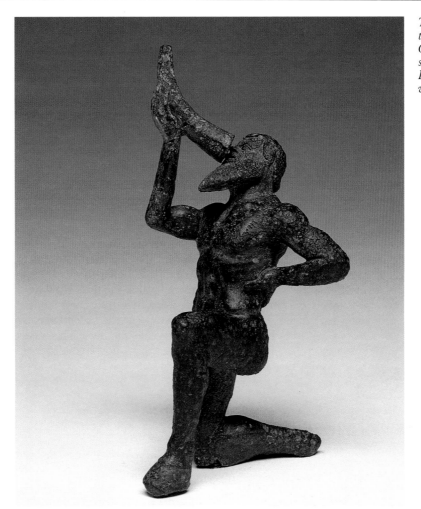

The drinking figure in this 5th-century-BC Greek statuette is a satyr, follower of Dionysus, god of the vine.

Greek papyrus from Egypt but it could equally have been a Roman dish: the ingredients are reminiscent of sauces found in *Apicius*.

Traditionally pork was salted not because of a flavour preference, but as the most economic way to preserve it for the winter: excess saltiness was then removed by the initial boiling specified in this recipe. Salted pork would hang in the fireplace in many ancient households.

Most of the flavourings listed are seeds, and we are not unfamiliar with roasting these, but why roast the herb thyme? The answer is simply that when thyme is dry-roasted the green leaves are easily removed from the stalk, making the herb easier to use.

Delian Sweets

'On Hecate's Island,' says Semus in Deliad II, *'the Delians sacrifice*
what they call basyniai *to Iris, goddess of the dawn. It is wheat dough,*
boiled, with honey and the so-called kokkora *(which are a dried fig and*
three walnuts).'
ATHENAEUS 645b

Another sweet: Take durum wheat flour and cook it in hot water so that it
forms a very hard paste, then spread it on a plate. When cold cut it up
in lozenges, and fry in best oil. Lift out, pour honey over, sprinkle with
pepper and serve.
Apicius 7, 11, 6

The first recipe is sketchy and difficult to interpret. Were the dried fig
and the walnuts ingredients in *basyniai*, or were they a separate offering to
the goddess? I believe that they were separate – so I offer them to guests
beside my Delian Sweets in order to remain loyal to the text. How were
the sweets themselves made? The Greek word here translated 'boiled'
could also mean 'fried', which does not help. But the second recipe,
quoted from *Apicius*, sheds light on a possible method. This gives
something remarkably like choux paste, though without the enriching
eggs and fat. In creating a modern version, therefore, I have kept choux
paste in mind.

MAKES ABOUT FIFTEEN

6 FL OZ (¾ CUP/170 ML) WATER

2 OZ (½ CUP/60 G) PLAIN (ALL-PURPOSE) FLOUR

OLIVE OIL FOR DEEP-FRYING

2 TABLESPOONS (60 G) HONEY

POPPY SEEDS OR FRESHLY GROUND BLACK PEPPER

Bring the water to the boil and add the sifted flour. Beat vigorously as if
you were making choux paste. Cook out for a few minutes and turn out on
to a large plate, or a marble slab if you have one. Allow to cool
completely. Heat the olive oil in a deep-fryer. Cut the paste into cubes: it
will be firm but still a little sticky. Test the oil for temperature with a little
of the mixture: if it rises and colours, the oil is ready. Drop the cubes in
the oil, 2 or 3 at a time. Cook for 3 to 4 minutes until golden-brown and
lift out on to kitchen paper. While they are still warm, dribble warmed

honey over the fritters and sprinkle them with either poppy seeds or freshly ground pepper.

Pepper was once very common as a seasoning for sweets. It is surprisingly good with honey. In our own tradition nutmeg has replaced pepper in dessert and sweet cookery, but nutmeg was practically unknown to the classical Greeks and Romans.

Women filling water-jugs: Athenian cup of about 400 BC.

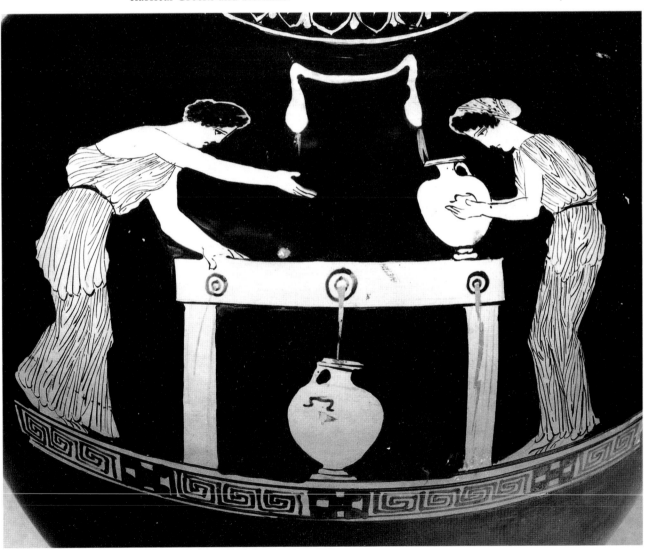

4

A WEDDING FEAST
IN MACEDON

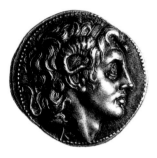

Alexander the Great, whose Eastern conquests brought new wealth to Macedonia and new food fashions to the Greek world.

Thanks to the skill and determination of Philip (*c.* 382–336 BC), and the boundless ambition and energy of his son Alexander the Great, Macedon grew in two generations from a backward kingdom on the northern fringes of Greece to a world empire.

Alexander died suddenly, in his palace in Babylon, in 323 BC. More than almost any other individual, he had changed the course of history. What was once the monolithic Persian Empire became, after Alexander, a group of Macedonian and Greek kingdoms stretching as far east as Afghanistan and the Indus valley. In Egypt, under its Macedonian dynasty, the literature of early Greece was systematically collected, became the subject of sustained and serious research, and was thus transmitted to Rome and later Europe. In Greek-ruled northern India the *Conversations of King Menander* with the philosopher Nagasena (second century BC), one of the great classics of Pali literature, would help to form the philosophy of Buddhism. Meanwhile the Greek language and 'Hellenistic' art and literature of the new kingdoms had a lasting influence of their own, on the later Near East and on the nascent culture of Rome. Greek would become the language of the New Testament, the first language of the new religion of Christianity. Without Alexander, the culture of much of the modern world would be vastly different.

From the point of view of Greece itself, Alexander's conquests brought immense wealth, new ideas – and new foods. Aristotle, Alexander's tutor, had encouraged him to take botanists and other scientists on his long journeys. The results, in terms of newly discovered fruits and vegetables, are recorded in the so-called *History of Plants* by Aristotle's successor, the scientist Theophrastus of Eresus. The Greeks who settled in Syria and Egypt experimented with new varieties of their own favourite food plants. The cooking skills of the East were ever more sought after in wealthy households: at the same time the cooking traditions of Greece spread eastwards.

We can begin to visualise the mixture of Greek, Macedonian and Near Eastern cultures that was taking place in the years after Alexander's death through an unusual narrative of about 300 BC that leads us into an

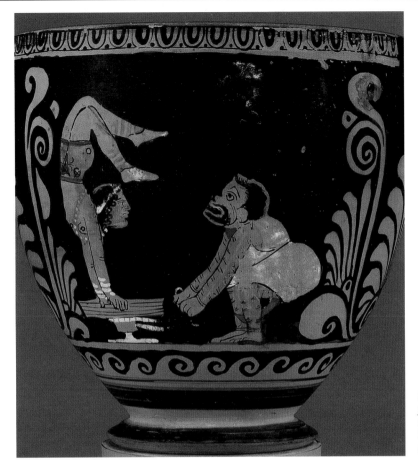

South Italian vase-painting, 4th century BC. A girl acrobat balances on a revolving wheel spun by a clown.

aristocratic Macedonian household at the moment of a wedding feast. Hippolochus, an Athenian, was one of the guests: his letter to Lynceus of Samos, describing the festivities, survives in the *Deipnosophists* of Athenaeus. Hippolochus and Lynceus, incidentally, were both students of Theophrastus.

'Twenty was the number of men invited,' Athenaeus tells us. We must take it that the women, even at this wedding feast, were celebrating separately! Each guest on arrival was given a silver drinking-cup – which, when he had drained it of wine, he was supposed to keep. Then, served on bronze plates, came flat loaves on which guests could heap morsels of chicken, duck and pigeon; then a second course, served on silver plates, with geese, hares and kids; and a third, with wood-pigeons, doves and partridges.

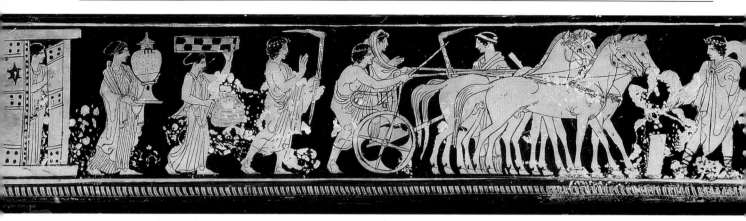

An Athenian wedding procession, depicted on a perfume-jar which was perhaps a wedding gift. By the 'Marlay Painter', about 440 BC.

We gave the slaves a share of this course, too [Athenaeus now quotes Hippolochus]; and when we had had enough eating we rinsed our hands. Lots of wreaths of all sorts of flowers were brought in, and gold circlets for all.

We were already far from sober when in rushed flute-girls and singers and some Rhodian harp-girls, I seem to think they were naked, only some have been saying they had tunics on. They did their act and went away. Then more girls trooped in each carrying a pair of half-pint flasks of perfume, one silver, one gold, yoked together with a golden strap, which they proffered to each of us.

Next was served something more like a treasure than a dinner! It was a silver dish (with quite a broad gold rim) big enough to take a whole roast porker, and a very large one too, which lay there on its back displaying all the good things its carcass was full of. Baked together inside it were thrushes and warblers, and yolk of egg poured over them. Barbecued oysters and scallops were served next, with a plate for each. After this we had a drink, and each of us was given a stewed kid on a silver dish, with gold spoons.

At last the second tables came in and fruit and nuts were offered to all in ivory baskets, and all sorts of cakes, Cretan and your very own Samian, my dear Lynceus, and Attic, with the receptacle proper to each.

The feast that Caranus, the bridegroom, had arranged for his friends was very different from anything that would have been seen in Greece in earlier times. The distribution of wreaths and perfumes was, admittedly, a Greek custom. But the quantities of food seem vast. There was far too much for any one person to eat. Yet it was not all wasted. Macedonian feasting enabled the guests to display their generosity to slaves and attendants and to take food home for their households. They were even given baskets to carry off the leftovers. And all the plates and utensils, gold, silver and bronze, were given to the guests to take away. Gift-giving was the method by which Macedonian kings had asserted their status and

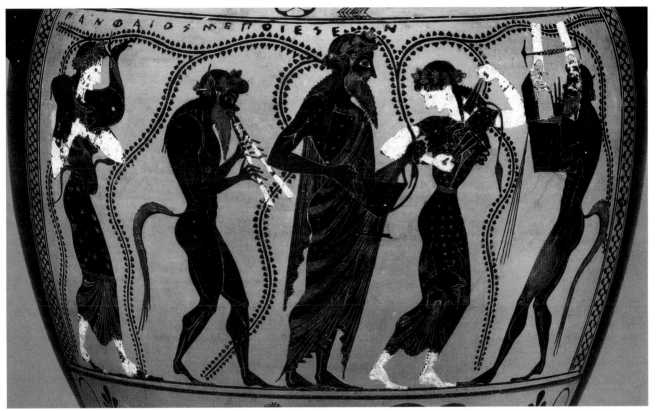

conducted their diplomacy. This, perhaps more than any other feature of the wedding feast, was a local custom, one that had no doubt suffered inflation thanks to the immense riches that Macedonians had now won in the East.

The recipes that follow are linked in one way or another with Macedon and its conquests. One of them comes from the Greek cookery book of which fragments were found among the papyri of Oxyrhynchus, in Egypt, where so much lost Greek literature has come to light. For the kid stew, the main course of the feast described by Hippolochus, we have substituted roast hare, a fine delicacy for a smaller-scale dinner and one of Greece's luxuries (for a recipe for roast kid or lamb, see page 36). The few surviving recipes for ancient Greek cakes and pastries include one of Cretan origin – Hippolochus actually mentions Cretan cakes – and one from Alexandria, the new Greek metropolis of Egypt that still bears the name of its founder Alexander.

Dionysus attended by a pipe-playing satyr and dancing maenad.

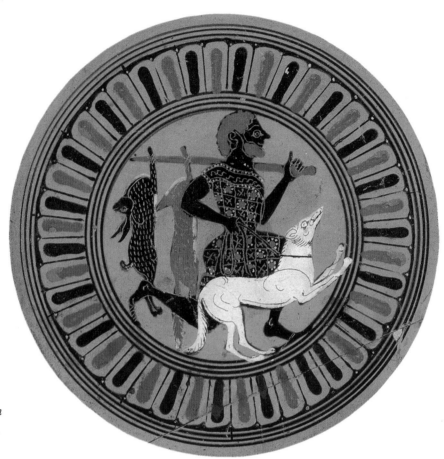

Successful huntsman and dog. At Athens hare was the typical game animal.

If we can judge by Caranus' feast, Macedonians did not look far afield for wine: he served Mendaean and Thasian vintages, from the Macedonian mainland and a neighbouring island. But they drank lavishly. Alexander's court was infamous for drunken quarrelling, sometimes fatal. Alexander, people said, had brought on his own death by over-indulgence in wine.

One of the best-known wines of modern Greece comes from Macedonia. The dry red of Naoussa, from the western hills, has a long history: Naoussa was already admired by travellers in the eighteenth century. There are also a red and a white Côtes de Meliton, from an estate south of ancient Torone. These latter wines, a blend of newly planted French and Greek varieties, cannot claim any historical tradition – but that would certainly not have worried Caranus or his guests.

Roast Hare

Drenched hare: it is first briefly scalded in water, then arranged in a pan. It is to be roasted in oil in the oven, and when nearly done more oil is to be added. Add the following sauce. Pound pepper, savory, onion, rue, celery seed, fish sauce, silphium, wine and a little oil. Turn a few times: let it finish cooking in this sauce.
Apicius 8, 8, 1

SERVES FOUR

1 SADDLE OF HARE

SALT

1 TEASPOON GROUND BLACK PEPPER

OLIVE OIL

2 SMALL ONIONS

2 TEASPOONS FRESH LOVAGE OR CELERY LEAF

1 TEASPOON DRIED SAVORY

2 TEASPOONS CHOPPED FRESH OR DRIED RUE

1 TEASPOON CELERY SEED

½ TEASPOON ASAFOETIDA POWDER OR 3 DROPS ASAFOETIDA TINCTURE

10 FL OZ (1¼ CUPS/280 ML) RED WINE

2 TABLESPOONS (30 ML) FISH SAUCE

Bring a large saucepan of water to the boil and either place the hare in the pan or pour the water over it to scald the meat briefly. Transfer the meat to a roasting tin and season well with salt and pepper and plenty of olive oil. Heat the oven to 375°F (190°C/gas mark 5) and roast the saddle for a total of 1½ hours.

Meanwhile prepare the sauce. Chop the onions finely and combine them with the other seasonings and the wine, fish sauce and 2 tablespoons (15 ml) olive oil. Remove the hare from the oven after 1 hour's cooking and add the sauce. Return to the oven for another 30 minutes, basting frequently with the sauce. When the meat is cooked, take it from the oven and keep it warm. Turn the sauce into a pan, bring to the boil and reduce slightly. Carve the meat and serve a little of the sauce on the side.

Hare can be found today at a specialist butcher or a market stall (rabbit may be used as an alternative). A whole hare will feed up to 6 people, and it is not usually sold in joints. The saddle is the best part of the animal: this is what you should use for the recipe. Ask your supplier to skin, draw and joint the hare for you; save the legs for another occasion. Hare is a very bloody meat and the process of scalding it in boiling water is useful to clean the meat before roasting.

The recipe from *Apicius*, used above, will probably be preferred by most readers. For a simpler view of the best way to deal with hare we can look back to the instructions of Archestratus: 'There are many ways, many rules for the preparation of hare. This is the best, that you should bring the roast meat in and serve to everyone while they are drinking: hot, simply sprinkled with salt, taking it from the spit while still a little rare. Do not worry if you see the blood seeping from the meat, but eat greedily. To me the other recipes are altogether out of place, gluey sauces, too much cheese, too much oil over, as if one were cooking a cat!'

Liver Oxyrhynchus

Cut up good liver, marinate in oil with salt, coriander, thyme, silphium,
opos, vinegar; grill on a spit at high temperature; serve.
Oxyrhynchus cookery book

SERVES TWO

8 OZ (225 G) LAMB'S LIVER

2 TABLESPOONS (30 ML) OLIVE OIL

2 TABLESPOONS (30 ML) RED WINE VINEGAR

1 LARGE HANDFUL OF CHOPPED FRESH CORIANDER

2 TEASPOONS DRIED THYME

GENEROUS QUANTITY OF SALT AND PEPPER

Carefully skin the liver and remove any sinews and blood vessels. Slice thinly and leave to marinate in the other ingredients for 2 to 3 hours or overnight. Line a grill (broiling) pan with cooking foil and place the liver slices on this with a little of the marinade. Grill (broil) at a high heat for 2 to 3 minutes on each side and serve with a little of the juice.

Baked Mackerel

COOK: 'Do you know how to cook horse mackerel?'
SLAVE: 'I will when you've told me.'
COOK: 'Take out the gills, rinse, cut off the spines all round, split neatly and
spread it out flat, whip it good and sound with silphium and cover with cheese, salt
and oregano.'
Alexis 138, quoted in ATHENAEUS 322c-d

SERVES TWO

2 MACKEREL

½ TEASPOON ASAFOETIDA POWDER OR 3 DROPS ASAFOETIDA TINCTURE

2 SPRIGS OF FRESH OREGANO

8 OZ (225 G) CHÈVRE CHEESE

SALT

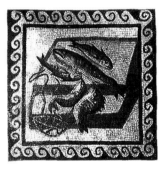

Remove the head from the mackerel and clean the fish. Split each fish all the way down its belly and open it out. Break the spine in 2 or 3 places with a heavy knife and lift out the bone. Remove as many of the little bones as you can. Spread it flat, flesh uppermost, in a greased baking dish. Sprinkle with the asafoetida powder or tincture. Chop the oregano roughly and combine with the crumbled cheese. Pack this mixture over the flesh of the fish, pressing it down carefully. Heat the oven to 350°F (180°C/gas mark 4) and bake the fish for 15 to 20 minutes until golden-brown and crisp.

Scad or horse-mackerel is not in fact a mackerel at all. It is a member of the *Carangidae* family, other members of which include bluefish and pilot fish. They all live in the warm waters of the Mediterranean; horse-mackerel alone is also found in British waters yet is rarely seen in fishmongers' shops. The fish is distinguished by prominent eyes and a stepped lateral fin. It is usually treated in the same way as mackerel, but is said by at least one authority to be not as good. I prefer to use mackerel for this recipe: it is easily available and well-flavoured.

Alexandrian Sweets

Itria: *thin sweetmeats made of sesame and honey.*
ATHENAEUS 646d

Harpocration of Mendes calls the Alexandrian kind of cake a pankapra.
This is crumbled itria *boiled with honey; and, when boiled, they are made
up into balls, wrapped in thin papyrus to hold them together.*
ATHENAEUS 648b

There are two kinds of itria, *the better kind called* ryemata *[flowed out]
and the poorer called* lagana *['wafer'].*
GALEN, *On the Properties of Foods* I, 4, I

Itria: *presents; nibbles; biscuity shapes.*
HESYCHIUS, *Dictionary*

These scraps of ancient writing give an example of the jigsaw puzzle from
which Greek and Roman foods sometimes have to be reconstructed. The
sweetmeats called *itria* are vaguely defined, but there is just sufficient information to develop a recipe. They could apparently be thin 'flowed-out' bis-
cuits (cookies) made of honey and sesame seeds. The honey was evidently
boiled as a first step: it is not so easy to see what processes followed.

The recipe following this one is for a more elaborate version of *itria*
known as *gastris*. There more detailed instructions specify roasting the
nuts before they are mixed with the honey, so there will be no need to add
heat a second time.

I have used the *gastris* method as a basis for the simpler *itria*. In both
the honey is boiled until it almost becomes caramel and sets in the same
way as toffee. The boiling time is crucial to the texture of the finished
sweet. Both sweets could be either crisp or chewy: we can see them as
ancestors of pralines or nougat.

I have enriched the *itria* with some nuts, in the belief that, despite lack
of evidence, the sweets of ancient Alexandria would have been as diverse
as our confectionery is today. You can be more adventurous and add
raisins, chopped dates or poppy seeds if you like.

MAKES ABOUT TWENTY PIECES

4 OZ (I CUP/I20 G) SESAME SEEDS

**3 OZ (¾ CUP/85 G) CHOPPED MIXED NUTS
(ALMONDS, WALNUTS, HAZELNUTS)**

6 OZ (¾ CUP/I70 G) CLEAR HONEY

78

Roast the sesame seeds and nuts in the oven at 350°F (180°C/gas mark 4) until they take on a little colour. Put the honey in a saucepan and bring to the boil, then skim and continue to simmer gently for 7 minutes. Add the nuts and sesame seeds to the honey while warm and mix well. Grease a shallow baking tray or dish and spread the mixture out on it. Allow to cool until you can handle the mixture and then mould into balls the size of boiled sweets. Wrap in little pieces of paper and serve with fruit and nuts at the end of a meal.

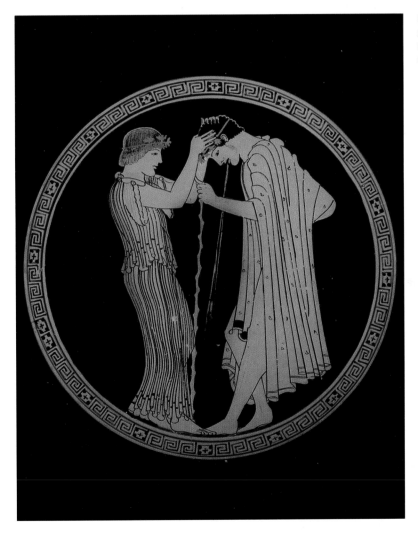

On the way home from the symposium: cup by the 'Brygos Painter', about 470 BC.

Honey Nut Cake

In Crete they make a little cake which they call gastris. *This is how it is done: sweet almonds, hazelnuts, bitter almonds, poppy seeds: roast them, watching them carefully, and pound well in a clean mortar. After mixing the nuts knead with boiled honey, adding plenty of pepper. It turns black because of the poppy. Flatten out into a square. Now pound some white sesame, work with boiled honey, and stretch two* lagana, *one below and the other above, so that the black is in the middle, and divide into shapes.*

Chrysippus of Tyana, quoted by ATHENAEUS 647f

MAKES ABOUT FIFTEEN PIECES

4 OZ (1 CUP/120 G) NIBBED ALMONDS

4 OZ (1 CUP/120 G) NIBBED HAZELNUTS

1 TABLESPOON (15 G) BITTER ALMONDS

2 TABLESPOONS (30 G) POPPY SEEDS

6 OZ (1½ CUPS/170 G) SESAME SEEDS

7 TABLESPOONS (210 G) CLEAR HONEY

**1 TEASPOON COARSELY GROUND BLACK PEPPER
(THIS MAY BE REDUCED IF YOU WISH)**

Heat the oven to 350°F (180°C/gas mark 4). Combine the nuts and poppy seeds and roast them to give them colour. Roast the sesame seeds briefly, allow them to cool, then pound or process them to a fine texture. Place 3 tablespoons (45 g) honey in a small pan, bring to the boil and simmer

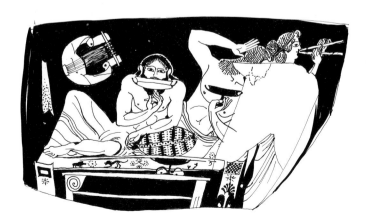

A drinker watches us: symposium scene on an Athenian krater *(wine-mixing bowl) of about 500 BC.*

80

gently for 7 minutes. Add the pounded sesame seeds and stir well. Allow to cool sufficiently to be touched and turn out on to a greased table or marble slab. Grease your hands and knead until firm but still warm. Divide into 2 equal portions and keep one of these warm on top of the stove. Grease a shallow square baking tray or pan with olive oil, then, using a greased rolling pin, roll out the cooler portion of sesame paste into a thin sheet to fit inside the tray.

Place all the roasted nuts in a food processor with the pepper and process for a minute or two till you have a fine texture. Boil the remaining 4 tablespoons (60 g) honey for 7 minutes in the same way as before, then add the nut mixture and stir well. While still hot, spread this over the sesame layer and level it off. Roll the second layer of sesame paste into a sheet that covers the nuts. Put it in place, leave for an hour to set and without further delay (or it will get too hard) cut into lozenges. Serve with fruit at the end of the meal, or as a sweet at any time.

Bitter almonds are obtainable from Chinese supermarkets. In small amounts they add an unusual tang to the recipe. You can find Greek mountain thyme honey in health-food stores and sometimes in supermarkets. Known as *thymeli*, it has a wonderful flavour and (though fairly expensive) adds a special touch to the sweet.

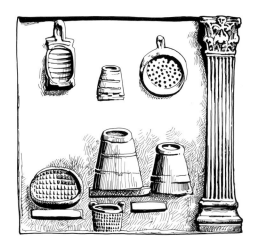

Flour sieves and storage receptacles from the bakery.

5
CATO'S FARM

For us Greek literature begins with the two great epic tales of heroes and their adventures. Roman literature begins in an utterly different way – with comic plays and a farming handbook.

The first full-length work of prose that happens to survive from Roman antiquity is a collection of notes jotted down as advice for someone who was planning to invest in a farm. The topics covered seem to be the ones that had concerned the writer himself: choosing a good business, keeping it profitable, managing slave labour.

Each time the master visits his farm, he will first greet the household spirit. Then he should go round the property – that very day, if he can; if not that day, the next. As soon as he is clear how the business stands, what jobs are finished and what is still to be done, next day he must send for the manager . . .

He must aim for best profit: sell oil when it will pay; sell surplus wine and grain; sell ageing oxen, less-yielding cows, less-yielding sheep; sell wool, hides, old carts, old tools, old slaves, sickly slaves, and anything else surplus. The master has to be a selling man, not a buying man.

The reader is told when and where to build a new farmhouse and how to equip it for wine and olive oil production. And, as a bonus for all who are interested in ancient food, there is a fascinating long section of recipes. These are not recipes for main dishes: you and your cook must work out your own choices for dinner. They are recipes for preserving meat and vegetables, for making cakes and sweets, for medicinal drinks and for special kinds of wine. They may seem to be a miscellaneous list, but they have something important in common. These are all items that could be made on the farm and kept for long-term use, or indeed sold at the nearest market. They give a unique snapshot of Roman farm economy long before Rome was the ruler of the world. Here is an example: 'How you should preserve lentils: dissolve silphium in vinegar, soak the lentils in the silphium-vinegar, and stand them in the sun. Then rub the lentils with oil, let them dry, and they will keep quite sound.'

This practical-minded author was one of the best-known figures of early Roman history. It is, in fact, quite remarkable that we have such a close insight into the way that an early statesman's mind worked when he

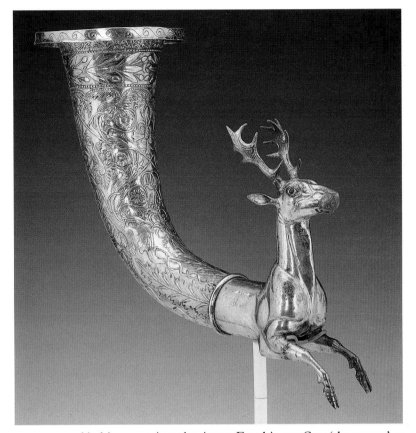

Silver-gilt drinking-horn, modelled as a stag, with inlaid glass eyes. From the Parthian Empire, Rome's eastern neighbour, modern Iraq and Iran.

was engaged in his own private business. For this was Cato 'the censor', a man of unusual foresight, unusual strictness, and unusual confidence in his own decisions. To later generations Cato was the typical traditional Roman. A fine military commander in Spain, a fine and honest governor of Sardinia, he had eventually been appointed censor back in Rome and, as such, had expelled some well-known men from the Roman Senate for lapses in morality: one of them, so it was said, for no other reason than that he had kissed his own wife while someone else was watching, the someone else being their daughter. Cato thinned the order of 'knights' too, Lucius Veturius being expelled because he was too fat to ride a horse. 'How can such a body be useful to the State,' Cato demanded, 'when everything between gullet and genitals has been taken over by stomach?'

Cato was also said to have a fierce aversion to the Greek culture that was then invading Rome and sapping the vigour of Roman youth. But in spite of such stories, he comes over in reality as severely practical.

As governor, he insisted, he would not be attended by a crowd of lackeys because it was a waste of the State's resources. As farmer, he would hold on to his olive oil until the price peaked, and he would keep slaves only while they were fit to work. Whatever he thought of the insidious dangers of Greek culture, Cato advised young Romans to learn Greek. Some of the wines for which he gives recipes are imitations of Greek wines. The cakes in his farming handbook have Greek names: they are a Roman version of Greek patisserie. If these wines and cakes would sell in Italian markets, Cato would make sure that his own farm drew some of the profits.

We know very little of Roman meals in Cato's time. As Rome came to dominate Italy, Sicily, Spain and southern France, the Romans certainly did learn to like the luxuries that were available in the old-established Greek cities in those regions. As Rome fought and defeated Carthage, the Carthaginian books on agriculture were officially translated into Latin: it is from one of these that Columella took his recipe for *passum* (raisin wine), mentioned earlier. Soon Romans would begin to make military conquests in the East. Greek slaves, including Greek cooks, would flood the city; Greek comedies, adapted into Latin, would sweep the Roman stage; and Greek ways of life and love would come to seem more natural than home-grown customs. Cato stands at the very beginning of these exciting developments.

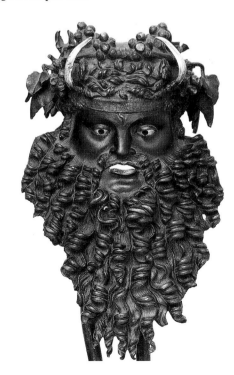

Mask of the wine god, Dionysus to Greeks, Bacchus to Romans, wreathed with grapes. Handle ornament of a Greek or Roman bronze bucket.

Even in Cato's time Greek wine was in fashion in Roman Italy. Why else should he give those complicated recipes for adding sea water to the must to imitate the wine of Cos?

Yet we can see from the firm and practical instructions for the vintage and the wine trade, elsewhere in Cato's handbook, that the wine of Italy was already big business. Two hundred years later the tireless Pliny tried to write the history of Italian vintages. In early times, he decided,

. . . no particular variety is famous, but one particular year is. *All* varieties gave of their best when L. Opimius was Consul, the very same year in which the Tribune C. Gracchus stirred up the people to rebellion and was assassinated. In that year, Rome's six hundred and thirty-third, the weather was ideally sunny – 'ripe', as people say. These Opimian wines have lasted about two hundred years already, though by now they have reduced to something resembling rough honey, evidently the natural state of wine in its old age. They are no longer drinkable by themselves, not even when diluted with water: their formidable maturity has at length turned to bitterness. They are 'medicines' now, used in tiny doses to improve other wines.

This marvellous year for Italian wines was 121 BC. Ancient wines did not usually last as long as two hundred years! As Pliny remarked in a later section of his encyclopaedia: 'No investment gains faster than wine up to its twentieth year, or loses faster after that – unless its price rises.' This may sound like self-contradiction, but the meaning is clear: wine that lasted longer than twenty years was a rarity. With the simple Roman dishes of this chapter, drink young Italian wines.

Garlic Cheese

First, lightly digging into the ground with his fingers, he pulls up four heads of garlic with their thick leaves; then he picks slim celery-tops and sturdy rue and the thin stems of trembling coriander. With these collected he sits before the fire and sends the slave-girl for a mortar. He splashes a grass-grown bulb with water, and puts it to the hollow mortar. He seasons with grains of salt, and, after the salt, hard cheese is added; then he mixes in the herbs. With the pestle, his right hand works at the fiery garlic, then he crushes all alike in a mixture. His hand circles. Gradually the ingredients lose their individuality; out of the many colours emerges one – neither wholly green (for the white tempers it), nor shining white (since tinted by so many herbs). The work goes on: not jerkily, as before, but more heavily the pestle makes its slow circuits. So he sprinkles in some drops of Athena's

olive oil, and adds a little sharp vinegar, and again works his mixture together. Then at length he runs two fingers round the mortar, gathering the whole mixture into a ball, so as to produce the form and name of a finished moretum. *Meanwhile busy Scybale has baked a loaf. This he takes, after wiping his hands . . .*
Moretum 88–120

Not for the faint-hearted, this fiery *moretum* (garlic cheese). If we take the poet's recipe at face value, it may include fifty cloves of garlic: a pretty powerful mixture, but surprisingly good with a fresh warm loaf and a few olives. The farmer has just a small ball of hard cheese in his larder yet the finished garlic cheese is described as firm enough to make a ball itself. The garlic is quite juicy when pounded and this determines how much cheese is to be used to produce a finished *moretum*. The olive oil and vinegar soften the mixture slightly but do not turn it into a spread.

SERVES SIX

2 HEADS (20–5 CLOVES) GARLIC

8 OZ (225 G) PECORINO ROMANO CHEESE

1 LARGE HANDFUL OF CORIANDER LEAVES

2 TEASPOONS CHOPPED FRESH RUE (OR DRIED IF NECESSARY)

2 HEAPED TEASPOONS CHOPPED FRESH CELERY LEAF

1 TEASPOON SALT

1 TABLESPOON (15 ML) WHITE WINE VINEGAR

1 TABLESPOON (15 ML) OLIVE OIL

Peel and roughly chop the garlic. Grate the cheese. Roughly chop the herbs. If you are grinding by hand, start with the garlic and salt; break it down to a pulp, then add the cheese and herbs. When you have a smooth mixture add the liquids and mix well. Gather the mixture together and chill. If you are using a food processor, add all the solid ingredients and process until the mixture is smooth in texture, then add the liquids. Serve with a crusty loaf as a snack.

The poem *Moretum* is sometimes attributed to Virgil, author of Rome's national epic, the *Aeneid*. The extract quoted here deserves to be a very famous one: it actually provides one of the national mottoes of the United States, '*E pluribus unum*' ('Out of the many, one'), a memorable phrase first used of the green herbs and white garlic of a ploughman's lunch!

OPPOSITE *Mosaic from Pompeii. Probably based on a painting, this seems to show a scene from Graeco-Roman comedy – it might be the title-scene of Menander's* Synaristosai, *'Women at Lunch'.*

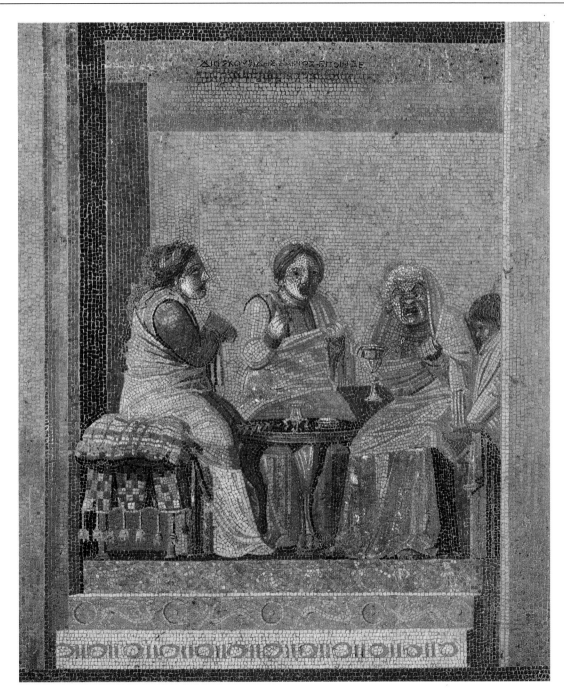

Moretum paints a picture of a poor peasant farmer struggling to make his living. The battle to survive is depicted in epic style, like a hero's quest. He is making his morning meal in the cold and damp of the dawn. He struggles to rekindle the fire in his draughty hovel; he strains to grind his meagre supply of wheat into flour, so that his wife can make their flat unleavened bread in the hearth.

Greeks and Romans used a mortar for grinding and mixing sauces. In this case the farmer would have used a large, coarsely made bowl with a grainy texture that helped to break down the ingredients. If you have a food processor, the effort required to produce the dish is minimal. If, on the other hand, you have to grind by hand you will need a large pestle and mortar. You can also gain first-hand experience of the suffering that the Roman farmer endured as he worked: 'Every so often the acrid smell assails his flaring nostrils and the farmer curses his meal, screwing up his face like a monkey. Now and then he wipes his smarting eyes with the back of his hand, swearing at the blameless fumes.'

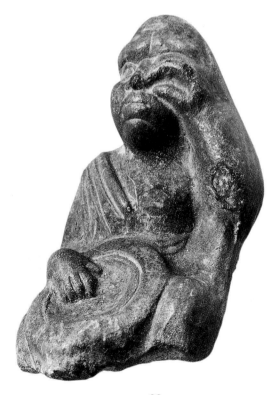

Chopping onions or garlic? Terracotta statuette of a slave with eyes streaming.

Lentils

*Lentils: boil, and when they have frothed add leek and coriander leaf.
Coriander seed, pennyroyal, asafoetida root, mint and rue; moisten with
vinegar, add honey, blend with fish sauce, vinegar, concentrated must, add
oil, stir. Adjust as needed. Bind with starch, add green oil on top, season
with pepper and serve.*

Apicius 5, 2, 3

SERVES SIX

8 OZ (225 G) GREEN LENTILS

2 SMALL LEEKS (WHITE PARTS ONLY)

1 LARGE HANDFUL OF FRESH CORIANDER

2 TEASPOONS CHOPPED FRESH MINT OR 1½ TEASPOONS DRIED MINT

1 TEASPOON CHOPPED FRESH OR DRIED RUE

GROUND BLACK PEPPER

2 TEASPOONS GROUND CORIANDER

2 GOOD PINCHES ASAFOETIDA POWDER OR
5 DROPS ASAFOETIDA TINCTURE

2 TABLESPOONS (30 ML) RED WINE VINEGAR

1 TABLESPOON (30 G) HONEY

3 TABLESPOONS (45 ML) FISH SAUCE

1 TABLESPOON (15 ML) DEFRUTUM (REDUCED GRAPE JUICE)

1 TABLESPOON (15 ML) OLIVE OIL

Soak the lentils in cold water overnight. Next day rinse them well in fresh
cold water and place them in a saucepan with enough water barely to
cover. Bring to the boil, skim if necessary and simmer gently. Chop the
leeks and fresh coriander and add to the lentils. Combine the mint, rue,
1 level teaspoon ground black pepper, the ground coriander and
asafoetida and add along with the liquids. Cook out until the lentils are
tender. You will not find it necessary to thicken the mixture as the
original recipe describes. Transfer to a serving dish and sprinkle with
olive oil and pepper.

Smoked Sausages (Lucanicae)

*Lucanicae similarly: crush pepper, cumin, savory, rue, parsley, mixed
herbs, bay berry, fish sauce, and mix in well-beaten meat, rubbing it well
into the mixture. Then, adding fish sauce, whole peppercorns, plenty of fat,
and pine kernels, stuff into an intestine (pulled as thin as possible) and
hang in the smoke.*
Apicius 2, 4

Lucanicae were traditionally smoked above the fireplace and not
otherwise cooked. This is no longer possible in the home, but we can still
give them a smoky flavour before grilling them. If you have an open
fireplace, they can be suspended from the mantelpiece for a few hours
while you burn wood. Alternatively you can use your barbecue: sprinkle
wood chips over the coals and suspend the sausages at least 12 in (30 cm)
above the fire for an hour or so.

SERVES SIX

1 LB (450 G) BELLY PORK, MINCED (GROUND)

2 TABLESPOONS (30 G) PINE KERNELS

20 BLACK PEPPERCORNS

1 TEASPOON CHOPPED FRESH OR DRIED RUE

2 TEASPOONS DRIED SAVORY

1 HEAPED TEASPOON GROUND CUMIN

1 TEASPOON GROUND BLACK PEPPER

30 BAY BERRIES (IF AVAILABLE)

2 TEASPOONS CHOPPED FRESH PARSLEY

3 TABLESPOONS (45 ML) FISH SAUCE

SAUSAGE SKINS

Combine all the filling ingredients and mix well: use a food processor if
available. If you have fresh skins, they will be preserved in salt and will
need to be washed. You will need about 6 × 12-in (30-cm) lengths. Tie a
knot in the end of each one. Put a ½-in (1-cm) plain tube in a piping bag
and half-fill with the mixture; do not put too much in at a time or it will be
difficult to squeeze. Take the open end of the skin, pull it over the tube
and push it down repeatedly until the majority of the skin sits like a collar
half-way down the tube. Grip this with your finger and thumb and slowly

release the skin as you squeeze the bag. Stop squeezing well before the skin has run out, leaving 2–3 in (5–7.5 cm) of skin to allow for shrinkage. It will take some practice before you get this procedure right. When you have used up all the meat, twist each length of sausage into 4 even segments. If you are able to smoke them, drape them over a coat-hanger or similar item and suspend in the smoke. Otherwise cut them into individual sausages and grill them under a medium heat.

Sausage skins can be bought freshly made from animal gut; synthetic skins are also available. An independent butcher, who makes his own sausages, will be able to help. You will need the chipolata-size skin. There is no need for an elaborate sausage-stuffing machine: a piping bag and a ½-in (1-cm) icing tube are quite adequate.

This is the most influential of all Roman recipes! The idea was brought back to Rome by soldiers who had served in Lucania, in the 'heel' of Italy, probably around Cato's time. Peppery, spicy, smoked sausages are still made in many parts of the world, from Palestine to Brazil, under names that can be traced back to *Lucanica*. In Brazil, for example, they are called *linguiça*. Recipes change with time, however, and the modern versions (even the Italian ones) contain few of the original ingredients.

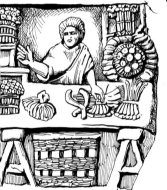

Greengrocer's shop. Relief carving from Ostia, Rome's harbour town at the mouth of the Tiber.

Celery Purée

Vegetable purée: boil celery in water with soda. Drain and chop finely. In a mortar crush pepper, lovage, oregano, onion, wine, fish sauce and oil. Cook in a saucepan and mix in the celery.

Apicius 3, 15, 2

SERVES FOUR

I CELERY HEAD

I MEDIUM ONION

5 FL OZ (⅔ CUP/150 ML) SWEET WHITE WINE

2 TABLESPOONS (30 ML) FISH SAUCE

I TABLESPOON (15 ML) OLIVE OIL

2 TEASPOONS CHOPPED FRESH LOVAGE OR 1 TEASPOON LOVAGE SEEDS

2 TEASPOONS CHOPPED FRESH OREGANO

½ TEASPOON GROUND BLACK PEPPER

Chop the celery roughly and wash it carefully. Chop the onion. Place both in a saucepan with water and bring to the boil. Cook until tender and drain. Place the wine, fish sauce and oil in a saucepan and add the herbs and pepper. Cook out gently for a few minutes. Purée the celery in a food processor or pass it through a metal sieve. Add to the sauce; heat together and serve.

This is excellent as a vegetable accompaniment for many of the meat and fish dishes in this book and can also be made with other vegetables. I have tried it with leek, cabbage and spinach with success. When making it with celery, if you do not have access to fresh lovage you can substitute 1 teaspoon lovage seeds: these can be found in Indian supermarkets. Celery leaf, which would normally work as a replacement for lovage, would be lost in this recipe.

Cheesecake

Libum *to be made as follows: 2 lb cheese well crushed in a mortar; when it is well crushed, add in 1 lb bread-wheat flour or, if you want it to be lighter, just half a pound, to be mixed well with the cheese. Add one egg and mix all together well. Make a loaf of this, with leaves under it, and cook slowly in a hot fire under a brick.*
CATO, *On Agriculture* 75

Libum means 'cake'. What kind of cake? It is often talked of by Roman poets, but what they say does not always match Cato's recipe. *Libum* was sometimes a sacrificial cake such as was offered to household spirits in the early years of Roman history; it was sometimes a farmhouse cake, served hot; it was sometimes a delicate honeyed cake that was served at the very end of an elaborate Roman dinner. The poet Ovid (43 BC–AD 18), writing of Roman religious festivals, tells us some tantalising details. He talks of a *libum* infused with clear honey – and he traces the origin of these cakes all the way back to mythology, and to the discovery of honey by the god Bacchus. Perhaps these particular cakes are included in Cato's farming book for religious reasons – to appease the gods, or to ensure the farm's fertility. *Libare*, after all, meant 'to offer to the gods'.

All the ancient writers associate *libum* with honey – all except Cato, and he is the only one who actually gives a recipe. His *libum* works perfectly well without honey. Cato's *libum* is a delicious savoury cheesecake, very successful when served hot. The cheese that is used can be quite salty and mature (I used feta) and the resulting texture, with golden-brown crust and soft centre, is similar to that of a modern baked cheesecake.

If, on the other hand, we take it that the proper thing was to add honey, a soft unsalted cheese must be chosen: the combination of salty cheese and honey is unappetising. Therefore, two recipes are given here. These cheesecakes, either sweet or savoury, will need to be baked under a *testum*, or baking brick: see Barley Rolls (page 53) for a full explanation.

Sweet Cheesecake

SERVES FOUR

4 OZ (1 CUP/120 G) PLAIN (ALL-PURPOSE) FLOUR

8 OZ (225 G) RICOTTA CHEESE

1 EGG, BEATEN

BAY LEAVES

4 OZ (½ CUP/120 G) CLEAR HONEY

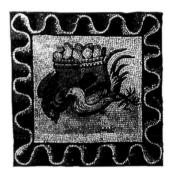

Sift the flour into a bowl. Beat the cheese until it is soft and stir it into the flour along with the egg. Form a soft dough and divide into 4. Mould each one into a bun and place them on a greased baking tray with a fresh bay leaf underneath. Heat the oven to 425°F (220°C/gas mark 7). Cover the cakes with your 'brick' and bake for 35 to 40 minutes until golden-brown. Warm the honey and place the warm cakes in it so that they absorb it. Allow to stand for 30 minutes before serving.

Savoury Cheesecake

SERVES FOUR

1 LB (450 G) FETA CHEESE

4 OZ (1 CUP/120 G) PLAIN (ALL-PURPOSE) FLOUR

1 EGG

2–3 BAY LEAVES

This is ideally made in a food processor. Break up the feta and place in the bowl. Process for 30 seconds until the mixture is smooth. Add the sifted flour and the egg and process for a few seconds until you have a soft dough. Mould into a loaf and shape into a slightly flattened circle. Score the top with 3 lines that divide the loaf into 6. Heat the oven to 425°F (220°C/gas mark 7). Place 2–3 fresh bay leaves under the loaf, cover with your 'brick' and bake for 45 to 50 minutes. Serve while still warm as an accompaniment to a first course or to a savoury course.

Layered Cheesecake

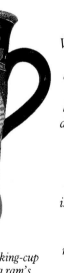

Athenian drinking-cup in the form of a ram's head; a drinking-party is depicted on the neck. 'Syriskos Painter', about 480 BC.

Placenta *to be made thus: 2 lb bread-wheat flour to make the base; 4 lb flour and 2 lb semolina to make the layers. Turn the semolina into water. When it is really soft, put it in a clean mortar and drain well; then knead it with your hands, and when it is well worked add the 4 lb flour gradually and make into sheets (*tracta*); arrange them in a basket to dry. When they are dry, rearrange them neatly. In making each sheet, when you have kneaded them, press them with a cloth soaked in oil, wipe them round and damp them. When they are made, heat up your cooking fire and your brick. Then moisten the 2 lb flour and knead it; from this you make a thin base.*

Put in water 14 lb sheep's cheese, not bitter, quite fresh; let it steep, changing the water three times; take it out and squeeze it gradually dry with the hands; when properly dry put it in a mortar. When all the cheese is properly dried out, in a clean mortar knead it with the hands, breaking it down as much as possible. Then take a clean flour sieve and press the cheese through the sieve into the mortar. Then add 4½ lb good honey and mix it well with the cheese. Then put the base on a clean table which gives a foot of space, with oiled bay leaves under it, and make the placenta.
First place a single sheet over the whole base, then, one by one, spread the sheets with the cheese and honey mixture from the mortar and add them to the placenta, *spreading them in such a way that you eventually use all the cheese and honey, and on the top put one more sheet by itself. Then draw up the edges of the base, having previously stoked up the fire. Then place the* placenta, *covered with the hot tile, and put hot coals around and above it. Be sure to cook it well and slowly. Open it to check on it two or three times. When it is cooked, remove it and coat in honey. This makes a 1-gallon* placenta.

CATO, *On Agriculture* 76

This remarkable cake also comes from Cato's farming book. The name is Greek (and it had nothing to do with the modern meaning of placenta, invented by a seventeenth-century scientist). In Greek the word could often mean a flat cake with a pastry base; goat's milk cheese and honey were among typical ingredients. A Greek comedy included a brisk exchange between a wordy gourmet and a down-to-earth eater:

'The streams of the tawny bee, mixed with the clotted river of bleating she-goats, placed upon a flat receptacle of the virgin daughter of Zeus, delighting in ten thousand delicate toppings – or shall I simply say cake?'
'I'm for cake.'

Roman *placenta*, like *libum*, was not only a delicacy for humans but also a sacrificial cake offered on temple altars. The Roman poet Horace tells of a temple slave who ran away because he was sick of honeyed *placenta* and wanted some good plain bread.

Cato's Latin *placenta* is a single, very specific and very complicated recipe. It is likely that Cato was confused by the recipe he was copying. The ratio of ingredients doesn't always work: the 2 lb of soaked semolina will not absorb 4 lb of flour to make a dough for the internal layers; and the base dough, when rolled out, will be several feet across! The thickness of the outer covering is crucial: if made to Cato's recipe, it must have been fairly thick or the cake would have been too large to bake. To make a dinner-party *placenta* we had better ignore the ratios he gives and simply follow the method.

The following recipe, then, is a small delicate version of Cato's cake that could have graced a Roman banquet.

SERVES SIX

2 OZ (⅓ CUP/60 G) SEMOLINA

6 OZ (1½ CUPS/170 G) PLAIN (ALL-PURPOSE) FLOUR

12 OZ (340 G) RICOTTA OR FULL-FAT CREAM CHEESE

3 TABLESPOONS (90 G) PLUS 8 OZ (1 CUP/225 G) CLEAR HONEY

BAY LEAVES

Place the semolina in a bowl with enough cold water just to cover it. Allow to stand for 1 hour. Sift 4 oz (¾ cup/120 g) flour into a bowl and form a dough with about 2 tablespoons (30 ml) cold water. Knead well and allow to rest. Strain the semolina and remove as much of the water as possible; place in a bowl and knead in 2 oz (⅓ cup/60 g) flour. Form a dough and leave to rest. Beat the cheese, add 3 tablespoons (45 g) honey and leave to one side. Divide the semolina dough into 6 equal pieces. Roll

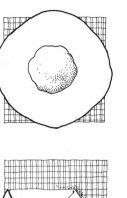
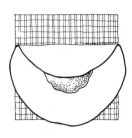
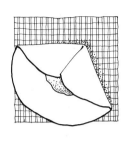
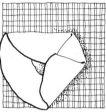
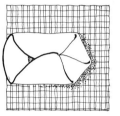
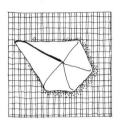

Steps in folding the pastry for the placenta.

out each one into a circle roughly 8 in (20 cm) across. Take a cake tin or ring of that size and cut each circle into a uniform shape. Carefully lay them on a lightly floured table to rest. Take the flour and water dough and roll it out with plenty of flour into a circle about 18 in (45 cm) across. About half-way through switch to using the back of your hands to pull the dough out. It should resemble strudel paste in thickness.

Now you can begin to build the cake. Grease a large baking tray with olive oil and place 3 or 4 large fresh bay leaves on it. Carefully lift the large flour-dough base on to the baking tray and let it drape over the edge. Place one layer of the semolina pastry on the base and put a tablespoon (15 g) of the honey mixture on this: spread it out to cover the whole area. Repeat until you have used up the honey and cheese; finish with a layer of pastry. Your pastry base should have at least 5 in (13 cm) of dough each side of the stack of honey layers. Standing before the cake, pick up the far edge of the base and pull it towards you and place it across the top layer. Move your hand down to the right and pull another part of the edge towards the centre; this will create a fold which you can repeat all round the cake. The final edge needs to be tucked in. Gather the pastry at the top and twist it off, leaving a small knob. Warm the remaining honey and liberally brush the cake all over. Cover with your 'brick' and bake in a pre-heated oven at 425°F (220°C/gas mark 7) for 45 minutes to 1 hour until golden-brown and crisp around the edge. Allow to cool slightly and place in a large dish with a lip. Pour the rest of the warmed honey over the cake and allow it to soak in for 30 minutes. Serve warm.

6

THE WEALTH OF EMPIRE

Cato, old-fashioned puritan though he seemed to many later Romans, marks a continuing trend. In the days of empire, even a moderately well-off Roman liked to talk of his country farm. He would hint at the wonderfully fresh produce that the farm manager and his wife had sent down to Rome that very day, a treat for the master and his dinner guests. The satirical poet Juvenal (born AD 67) pushes the fashion to the edge of ridicule:

Listen to the menu: no market stuff here. A fine plump kid, the most tender of the herd, from my farm at Tivoli, so babyish it has more milk in its veins than blood; wild asparagus gathered by the manager's wife after her spinning; big warm eggs wrapped in straw; and their mothers[!]; and grapes preserved half a year but just as good as when they were fresh; and Signine pears and Syrian pears and apples fresh-scented from their harvest baskets, rivals of the Picentine and nothing for you to fear, cured by the autumn chill of any dangerous roughness in their juice.

How different from classical Athens! There the boast was of produce one had found on the market, and of the haggling over the price.

We have moved forward in time two hundred years. Rome, once a country town in central Italy, is now the centre of a world state. Traditionally guided by aristocrats, eventually broken apart by the unbounded ambitions of Julius Caesar (100–44 BC) and others, Rome has crumbled into anarchy. Caesar's adopted son, Octavian (63 BC–AD 14), has under the name of Augustus been accepted as *princeps*, the 'first man' of the republic; his authority has passed to his own stepson and adopted son, Tiberius (42 BC–AD 37), and republic has somehow turned into empire.

Romans taxed the whole Mediterranean world, and could afford to buy their luxuries from anywhere in the empire – and beyond. The spices of India and Indonesia crossed the ocean, bound for Rome, and Roman gold went eastwards to pay for them.

Rome had grown fearfully rich – but still retained the power to laugh at herself. Juvenal was only one of the great satirists of that first hundred years of empire. Another, apparently friend and courtier of Nero (AD 37–68) himself, was the novelist Petronius. His *Satyricon* drew a portrait of a whole world, the new rich and the work-shy poor, the slave, the lecturer, the prostitute and the vast landowner. Or so it seems. All too little of the *Satyricon* survives, but the centrepiece of what remains is a lavish dinner, 'Trimalchio's Feast', a mockery of the wealth and pretension of imperial Italy. The narrator, Encolpius, is an educated vagabond who has managed to get himself an invitation:

Now some really high-class appetisers came in. We had all got on our couches by this time – only our host was still missing. Trimalchio was going to take the place of honour *himself*. Latest fashion? Anyway, on the trolley there was a Corinthian bronze donkey with panniers on its back, green olives in one, black in the other. Over the top of the donkey were two trays. Along the edge of them it said: 'Property of Trimalchio' and '*x* pounds silver'. These two dishes were joined together by little bridges soldered on, and they contained dormice glazed in honey and rolled in poppy seeds. There were sizzling sausages, too, on a silver grill – and, under the grill, damsons and pomegranate seeds.

As in a second-rate restaurant, the effort went into display: the food was showy and expensive (Roman cuisine, thanks to this episode, will be forever associated with dormice glazed in honey and rolled in poppy seeds), but not especially good. Encolpius and his disreputable friends crept away at midnight, leaving Trimalchio still drinking.

For better or worse 'Trimalchio's Feast' is the fullest description of a Roman dinner-party that we can now read. Luckily there is plenty of other evidence from which we can build up a picture of the usual routine.

As in Greece, many houses had a special dining room, the *triclinium*. Three couches, each large enough for three diners, were arranged in a U-shape surrounding a central table. A house with a big enough garden might well have a garden dining area, too, shaded by vines and creepers, with three stone couches sloping gently upwards to the middle – to be made comfortable with cushions and pillows. The open side of the square was for waiters to come and go.

Roman women and children had never dined separately from the menfolk as in Greek families. In the old days, it was said, they sat demurely at the foot of their husband's or father's couch; by the time of the empire they had become used to reclining. Servants took off guests' sandals as they reclined, and brought water to wash their hands. A sequence of dishes began with the *gustatio*, appetisers or *hors d'oeuvres*, followed by a sweet aperitif (see the first recipe in this chapter). These appetisers might be more varied and more costly than the main course, though not so bulky. We know of a religious dinner, attended by Julius Caesar, at which sixteen *hors d'oeuvres* awaited the priestly celebrants. They ranged from sea-urchin and clams to venison and wild boar.

OPPOSITE *A busy banquet scene: wall-painting from Pompeii. A slave removes a guest's sandals, and a friend offers a cup of wine. Another guest, who has eaten or drunk too much already, is helped away.*

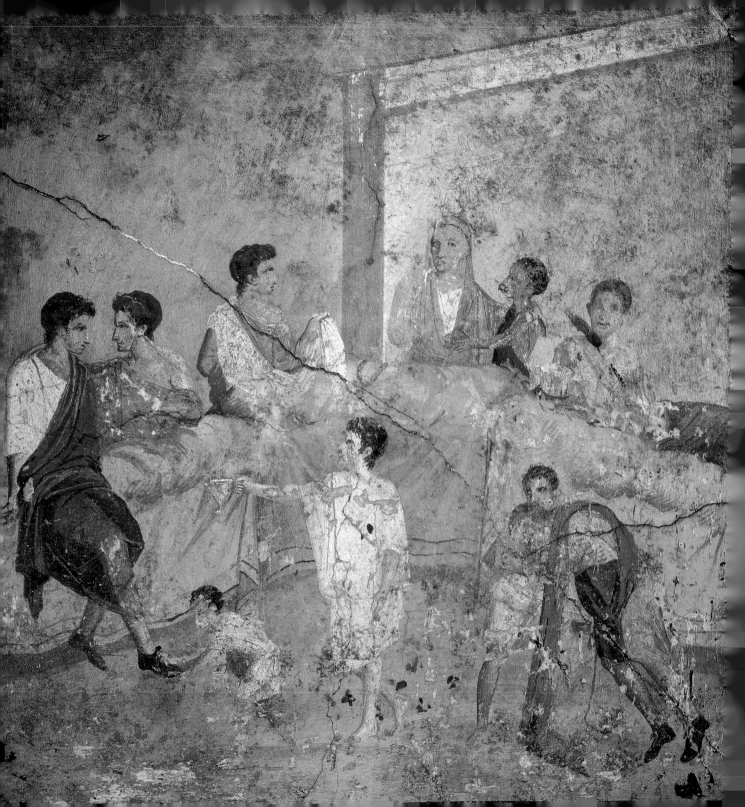

The main courses were accompanied by bread and wine. Servants must have been forever coming and going, bringing new courses, clearing away, supplying more perfumed water for finger-rinsing: for diners ate with their hands, with the occasional help of a knife. Music and dance, performed by slaves, might well accompany the drinking, which tended to continue long after the meal itself was over. A napkin, which lay in front of the diners as they reclined, might serve as a knapsack to take home the little gifts of food or wine with which a host would regale his friends as they departed.

We have not quoted a long list of main courses – read Petronius' *Satyricon* for plenty of examples – but the impression may remain that a Roman dinner was an expensive affair. It seems right to end, therefore, with a letter in which Pliny the Younger (born *c.* AD 62; nephew of the encyclopaedist) teases a friend with a menu of the dinner-party that he missed.

Dear Septicius Clarus: You promise, but you don't turn up to dinner, I'm afraid! All ready and waiting were a lettuce (each), three snails, two eggs, porridge, with *mulsum* and snow (yes, I must count in the snow, right away, because it melted on the plate), olives, beetroot, gourds, bulbs and a thousand other things no less enviable. You could have listened to comic actors or a poetry reader or a lyrist, or, such is my generosity, all three. But you chose to go to someone else's, and what did you get? Oysters, sows' wombs, sea-urchins, and dancing-girls from Cadiz!

By the early empire – a hundred and fifty years after the famous Opimian vintage – the wines of Italy were a serious study. Names like Caecuban and Falernian were famous in poetry. But wine snobbery led rich gourmets like Lucullus (117–66 BC) to prize the expensive, boiled-down, sweet export wines of Greece above their own. The custom grew of serving several kinds of wine in sequence at a single party. Pliny writes:

Greek wine was so prized that one would serve just one cup each at a dinner. 'As a boy,' Varro tells us, 'Lucullus never attended a banquet at his father's house at which more than a single cup of Greek wine was served. Well, on his own return from service in Asia Minor, Lucullus distributed more than a hundred thousand jars of Greek wine as gifts!' Caesar, at his triumphal dinner as dictator, provided an amphora of Falernian and a small jar of Chian to each table; but at the feast in his third consulship it was Falernian, Chian, Lesbian, Mamertine. That was the first time, apparently, that four kinds of wine were served.

'I'm giving you real Opimian,' Trimalchio boasted improbably at his dinner table. 'I didn't serve such good stuff yesterday, and my guests then were much better class.'

Spiced Wine

Making Conditum Paradoxum. *15 [lb] honey are put in a bronze jar
which already contains 2 pints wine, so that you boil down the wine as you
cook the honey. This to be heated over a slow fire of dry wood, stirring with
a stick as it cooks: if it begins to boil over it is stopped with a splash of
wine; in any case it will simmer down when the heat is taken away, and,
when cooled, re-ignited. This must be repeated a second and a third time;
then the mixture is finally removed from the brazier and, on the following
day, skimmed. Next 4 oz ready-ground pepper, 3 scruples mastic, 1 dram
each bay leaf and saffron, 5 roasted date stones, and the dates themselves
softened in wine to a smooth purée. When all this is ready, pour on 18 pints
smooth wine. If the finished product is bitter, coal will correct it.*

Apicius I, I

The Romans traditionally served a honeyed wine as an aperitif with the
first course at dinner. It was known as *mulsum* and was simply a mixture
of honey and wine in a ratio dependent on personal taste. The honey was
boiled so that it could be skimmed, but I find that this is less necessary
with modern honey. For *mulsum* add 4 oz (½ cup/120 g) clear honey to a
bottle of medium-dry white wine: warm the honey slightly so that it will
dissolve in the wine. Chill before serving.

The *Apicius* recipe, however, is for something finer: a special spiced
wine or *conditum*, distant ancestor of modern aperitifs such as Martini.
The recipe seems much too sweet, but the intended quantity of honey is
not clear in the manuscripts. A Greek recipe for *conditum* suggests a much
smaller proportion: 'Making *conditum*: washed, dried, finely ground

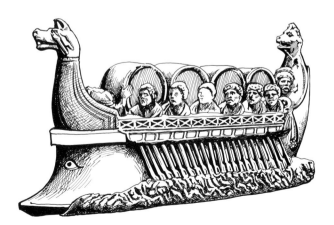

*In the Roman west,
wooden barrels were
the new way of storing
and transporting wine.
Model of a laden wine
ship found at
Neumagen in Roman
Germany.*

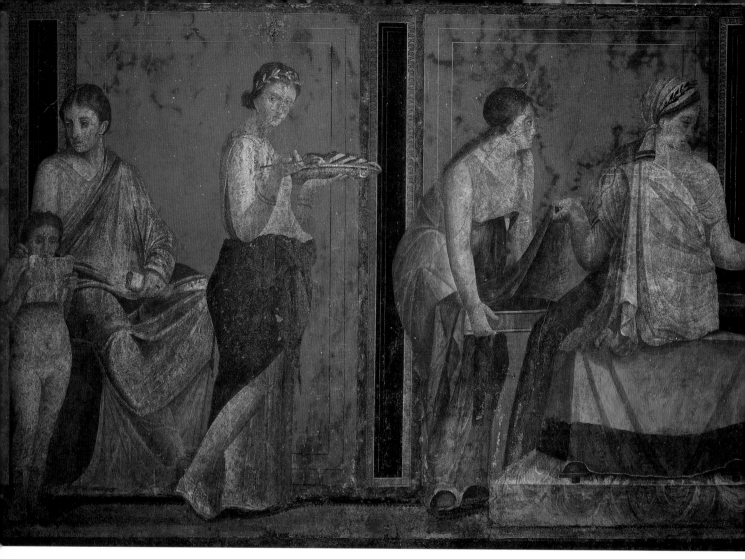

Detail of the 'Fresco of the Mysteries' from a villa near Pompeii. Women gather around a table; a slave brings a tray (of cakes?). Their trance-like faces remind the viewer that they are participating in a religious ceremony. Historians dispute its significance endlessly.

peppercorns, 8 scruples. Attic honey, 1 pint. Old white wine, 4 or 5 pints.' This is my excuse for reducing the quantity of honey considerably in the following recipe, though in other ways it is based on *Apicius*.

Mastic is a resin which has been exported from the Greek island of Chios for at least two thousand years. It has a very strong and distinctive flavour, familiar to many Greeks because traditionally they have chewed it to clean the teeth and freshen the breath. *Mastikha*, a spirit similar to ouzo but flavoured with mastic, is widely marketed in Greece. If you want to include mastic it can be bought from traditional herbalists such as Baldwin's in the UK (see page 24 for the address) or from Greek delicatessens.

MAKES SIX GLASSES

I BOTTLE (70 CL) MEDIUM-DRY WHITE WINE

6 OZ (¾ CUP/170 G) CLEAR HONEY

½ TEASPOON GROUND BLACK PEPPER

I BAY LEAF

PINCH SAFFRON POWDER OR STRANDS OF SAFFRON

PINCH MASTIC (OPTIONAL)

**I FRESH DATE, THE STONE ROASTED FOR 10 MINUTES
AND THE FLESH SOAKED IN A LITTLE WINE**

Put 5 fl oz (⅔ cup/150 ml) of the wine in a saucepan with the honey and bring it to the boil. Skim if necessary. Repeat and remove from the heat. Add the seasonings to the wine while it is hot: this speeds up the flavouring process. When it is cold, add the rest of the wine and allow to stand overnight. To serve, strain through a fine sieve or muslin.

Chicken Salad (Sala Cattabia)

Another, Apician sala cattabia: *put in a mortar celery seed, dried pennyroyal, dried mint, ginger, coriander leaf, seeded raisins, honey, vinegar, oil and wine. Crush. Put in a pan bits of Picentine bread, layered with chicken meat, kid's sweetbreads, Vestine cheese, pine kernels, cucumbers, dried onions chopped fine. Pour the liquid over. At the last moment scatter snow on top and serve.*

Apicius 4, 1, 2

There is an interesting combination of flavours and textures in this ancient salad, which is ideal as a first course. I think of it as one of the most successful dishes in *Apicius*. Lamb's sweetbreads are particularly suitable for the contrast of texture. The ancient method is a little vague: I settled on a completely lined mould, as for an apple charlotte or summer pudding, and turn it out before serving.

Vestine cheese was a smoked goat's milk cheese marketed by the Vestini, a mountain people of Abruzzo in central Italy, and it was one of Rome's delicacies. My choice of Pecorino Romano, a sheep's cheese very like Parmesan, is a personal one: it is dry with a pungent flavour that contrasts well with the other, milder, ingredients of the salad. You could use a mature Cheddar, or even fresh Parmesan.

Picentine bread, from the same region of Italy, was made in a special way. The recipe involves leaving soaked semolina to ferment for nine days before baking, and the earthenware pots in which the dough was placed broke in the oven in the course of baking. The bread, which was white and very light in texture, was always eaten soaked in milk or wine. Substitute a white, sliced, grain-enriched loaf. You will need a 2-pint (5-cup/1.2-litre) pudding basin or similar bowl to make the salad.

SERVES FOUR

8 SLICES GRAIN-ENRICHED WHITE BREAD

2 CHICKEN BREASTS, COOKED AND DICED

4 OZ (120 G) LAMB'S SWEETBREADS, COOKED AND DICED

3 OZ (85 G) PECORINO ROMANO CHEESE, GRATED

I MEDIUM ONION, FINELY DICED

4 TABLESPOONS (60 G) PINE KERNELS

½ CUCUMBER, PEELED AND FINELY SLICED

Dressing

I IN/2.5 CM FRESH ROOT GINGER, FINELY DICED

I LARGE HANDFUL OF FRESH CORIANDER

2 TABLESPOONS (60 G) RAISINS

I TEASPOON CHOPPED FRESH OR ½ TEASPOON DRIED MINT

I TEASPOON CHOPPED FRESH OR DRIED PENNYROYAL
(IF NOT AVAILABLE, INCREASE THE MINT)

I LEVEL TEASPOON CELERY SEEDS

3 TABLESPOONS (45 ML) RED WINE VINEGAR

5 FL OZ (⅔ CUP/150 ML) RED WINE

I TABLESPOON (30 G) HONEY

3 TABLESPOONS (45 ML) OLIVE OIL

SALT AND PEPPER

SPRIGS OF PARSLEY

Remove the crust from the bread and cut each slice into 3 oblong pieces. Line a 2-pint (5-cup/1.5-litre) pudding basin with the bread as for summer pudding and cut a circle of bread to put in the bottom. Prepare the salad ingredients. Place a quarter of the chicken meat in the bottom of the dish. Follow this with an equal amount of the sweetbreads, cheese, onion and pine kernels; add a layer of cucumber. Repeat until you have used up all the ingredients.

To prepare the dressing you will need a pestle and mortar. Pound the ginger, coriander and raisins to a pulp – this will take some time. Add the remaining herbs and celery seeds and mix well. Flush the mortar out with the vinegar and transfer to another bowl. Add the wine, honey, oil and seasoning. Pour this dressing over the salad and finish with a layer of cucumber. Cover with a saucer, place a weight on top and chill thoroughly. When ready to serve, release the bread from the edge of the dish with a palette knife and turn it out on to a plate. Decorate with cucumber slices and sprigs of parsley.

Stuffed Gourd

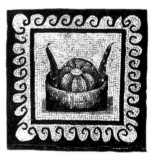

Stuffed gourd hors d'oeuvre. *Carefully cut oblong shapes from the sides of the gourds, hollow them out, put in cold water. Make the following stuffing for them: crush pepper, lovage, oregano, moisten with fish sauce, crush cooked brains, beat raw egg and add to make a smooth mixture: blend with fish sauce. Fill the aforesaid gourds, not fully cooked, with this stuffing, close them with the cut-out pieces, boil, drain when cooked, slice, fry. Make an* oenogarum *thus: crush pepper, lovage, moisten with wine and fish sauce, blend with raisin wine, put a little oil into the saucepan and let it boil. When it has boiled, bind with starch, pour the* oenogarum *over the fried gourds, season with pepper and serve.*
Apicius 4, 5, 3

Gourd is not easily available to us: marrow, squash and pumpkin, quite unknown to the Romans as they come from Central and South America, will serve as substitutes. Marrow and squash are seasonal vegetables, available from July to October, and should be chosen with care. Look for young ones, no more than 12 in (30 cm) long, with tender skin. As a first course this recipe is also successful with courgettes (zucchini). The stuffing is made with lamb's brains but minced (ground) lamb, or even beef, will do as well.

S ERVES S IX AS A S TARTER; T HREE OR F OUR AS A M AIN C OURSE

**I SMALL MARROW OR LARGE YELLOW SQUASH OR
4 COURGETTES (ZUCCHINI)**

OLIVE OIL FOR FRYING

Stuffing

8 OZ (225 G) LAMB'S BRAINS OR MINCED (GROUND) LAMB

I EGG

2 TEASPOONS CHOPPED FRESH LOVAGE OR CELERY LEAF

**2 HEAPED TEASPOONS CHOPPED FRESH OR
I½ TEASPOONS DRIED OREGANO**

2 TABLESPOONS (30 ML) FISH SAUCE

½ TEASPOON GROUND BLACK PEPPER

Sauce

5 FL OZ (⅔ CUP/I50 ML) RED WINE

2 TABLESPOONS (30 ML) FISH SAUCE

5 FL OZ (⅔ CUP/I50 ML) RAISIN WINE

2 TABLESPOONS (30 ML) OLIVE OIL

I TEASPOON CHOPPED FRESH LOVAGE OR CELERY LEAF

PLENTY OF GROUND BLACK PEPPER

A LITTLE CORNFLOUR (CORNSTARCH) TO THICKEN

Cut an oblong in the marrow, squash or courgettes, just as described in the ancient recipe above, and hollow out the flesh (keep the oblong cut-out). Push a spoon beyond the edges of the hole to make a large cavity, but do not break the skin. If you are using a marrow or squash and have a large enough saucepan, plunge the vegetable in boiling water for 10 minutes and refresh in cold water. If a large enough pan is not available, put the marrow or squash in a deep-sided ovenproof dish, pour in boiling water till it is half-covered, then cover with foil, bake in a pre-heated oven at 350°F (190°C/gas mark 4) for 20 minutes and refresh in cold water. There is no need to cook courgettes at this stage.

The lamb's brains should be soaked in cold water to remove any blood, trimmed of any fibres or bone and roughly chopped. Combine all the ingredients for the stuffing in a food processor and mix well. Stuff the marrow or squash, pressing the mixture into the hollowed-out ends. Replace the oblong cut-out and tie it securely with kitchen string. Return the vegetable to the saucepan, cover with water and simmer for 1 hour; alternatively place in a deep ovenproof dish with enough water to come half-way up the sides of the vegetable, cover with foil and bake in the oven at 400°F (200°C/gas mark 6) for a similar time. Courgettes will take no more than 30 minutes.

When cooked, drain and allow to stand while you combine the ingredients for the sauce. Bring them to the boil, simmer and reduce a little while you fry the stuffed vegetable. Remove the string and carefully cut into ¾-in (2-cm) slices. Heat olive oil in a frying-pan, place the slices in the hot oil and seal each side for 2 to 3 minutes. For a starter arrange 2 slices on a plate and spoon a little of the sauce over the meat.

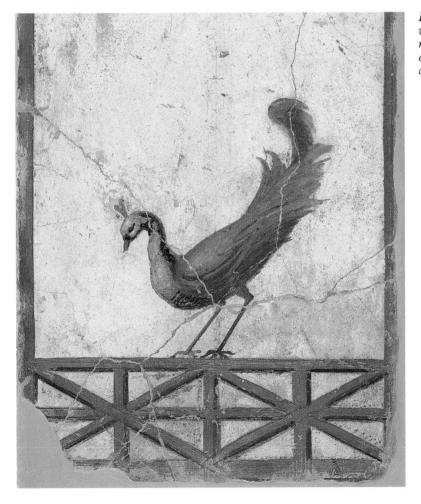

Peacock from a Roman wall-painting. Peacock meat, and peahen's eggs, were expensive delicacies.

Parthian Chicken

Parthian chicken. Open the chicken at the rear and spreadeagle. Crush pepper, lovage, a little caraway, moisten with fish sauce, blend with wine. Arrange the chicken in a Cuman dish and put the sauce over it. Dissolve strong asafoetida in warm water; pour over the chicken as you cook. Serve seasoned with pepper.

Apicius 6, 9, 2

SERVES FOUR

4 PIECES CHICKEN (BREAST OR LEG)

GROUND BLACK PEPPER

6 FL OZ (¾ CUP/170 ML) RED WINE

2 TABLESPOONS (30 ML) FISH SAUCE

½ TEASPOON ASAFOETIDA POWDER OR
5 DROPS ASAFOETIDA TINCTURE

2 TEASPOONS CHOPPED FRESH LOVAGE OR CELERY LEAF

2 TEASPOONS CARAWAY SEEDS

Place the chicken in a casserole dish and sprinkle it liberally with pepper. Combine the wine, fish sauce and asafoetida, add the lovage and caraway seeds and pour over the chicken. Cover and bake in a pre-heated oven at 375°F (190°C/gas mark 5) for 1 hour. Half-way through the cooking time remove the lid to brown the chicken. Serve with a little of the sauce poured over the meat.

This is a simple dish, and very unusual in a Roman context, for it contains no sweetener. It is interesting that it is named after Parthia, Rome's rival in the Middle East, and notable that asafoetida is the dominant flavour. This may confirm that the recipe was Parthian in origin – or at least it may explain how it got its name – for asafoetida came to Rome from the Parthian Empire. Caraway, on the other hand, is of central European origin. It was certainly the Romans who added this to the dish.

Green caraway, rather than caraway seed, was probably intended. However, caraway is difficult to obtain fresh unless you grow it in a greenhouse. I use the seed and find that it works very well.

Shoulder of Pork with Sweet Wine Cakes

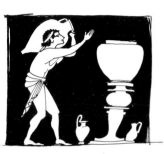

Wine in an amphora helps to fill the mixing bowl. Scene from a wine-jar by Smikros, about 505 BC.

Shoulder of pork with must cakes. Boil the cured pork with two pounds of barley and 25 dried figs. When it has boiled, take off the meat, singe its fat on a red-hot griddle and dip in honey. Better, put it in a bread-oven and coat it with honey. When it has browned, put in a saucepan raisin wine, pepper, a bunch of rue, wine; blend. When blended, pour half of this pepper sauce over the pork and the other half over bite-sized pieces of must cakes. When they have steeped, pour over the pork any that was not soaked up by the cakes.

Apicius 7, 9, 3

Must cakes to be made thus: two gallons of bread-wheat flour to be moistened with must; add to this anise, cumin, 2 lb lard, 1 lb cheese, and grate in the bark of a bay twig; when you have shaped them, put bay leaves under them while you cook them.

CATO, *On Agriculture* 121

This is an excellent dish for a special dinner: I have often prepared it for Roman banquets. The sweet wine cakes needed some thought. Fresh must begins to ferment almost as soon as it is pressed and can prove an effective leaven. I believe that, though no proving time is given, Cato's cook expects these cakes to rise. The grape juice that can be bought today in supermarkets is inactive and of no use here. I have experimented with wine with better results, but a really light and absorbent texture is not obtainable today without a little yeast.

SERVES SIX

Sweet Wine Cakes

8 OZ (2 CUPS/225 G) PLAIN (ALL-PURPOSE) FLOUR

2 OZ (2 TABLESPOONS/60 G) PASTRY LARD (SUCH AS COOKEEN)

2 OZ (60 G) PECORINO TOSCANO CHEESE, GRATED

1 TEASPOON GROUND CUMIN

1 TEASPOON ANISEED

3–4 TABLESPOONS (45–60 ML) RED WINE

BAY LEAVES

PINCH OF FRESH YEAST OR ½ TEASPOON DRIED YEAST

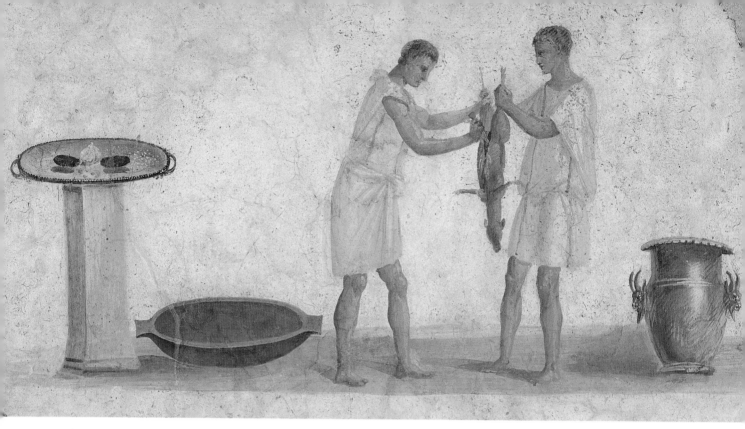

Preparing dinner. Slaves are gutting a fawn; a head of garlic is among the supplies awaiting use. Roman wall-painting, 1st century AD.

To make the sweet wine cakes, sift the flour and rub in the lard. Add the cheese, cumin and aniseed. Bring the wine, with one bay leaf, to body temperature and dissolve the yeast in it. Remove the bay leaf. Add the warm wine to the flour. Form a soft dough and knead well. Divide into 6 portions and mould each into a bun shape. Place on a greased baking tray with a bay leaf beneath each one. Cover with a cloth and leave to rest and rise in a warm place for 1½ hours. Bake in a pre-heated oven at 375°F (190°C/gas mark 5) for 25 to 30 minutes until risen and golden.

Gammon

1½ LB (675 G) PIECE OF GAMMON OR SMOKED HAM

8 OZ (2½ CUPS/225 G) PEARL BARLEY

10 DRIED FIGS

1 CELERY STALK

2 BAY LEAVES

10 PEPPERCORNS

8 OZ (1 CUP/225 G) HONEY

Sauce

10 FL OZ (1¼ CUPS/280 ML) RED WINE

10 FL OZ (1¼ CUPS/280 ML) RAISIN WINE

**2 TEASPOONS DRIED RUE IN A MUSLIN BAG OR
A GOOD SPRIG OF FRESH RUE**

½ TEASPOON GROUND BLACK PEPPER

Leave the meat soaking in cold water overnight. Discard the water and place the meat in a large saucepan, cover with fresh cold water and add the barley, figs, celery, bay leaves, peppercorns and 4 oz (½ cup/120 g) honey. Bring to the boil, skim and simmer for 1 hour. Pre-heat the oven to 400°F (200°C/gas mark 6). Remove the meat from the saucepan and retain the liquor. Cool the meat slightly before coating the fat with honey. Place in the oven for 30 minutes.

Meanwhile prepare the sauce. Place the wine, raisin wine and 5 fl oz (⅔ cup/150 ml) of the cooking liquor in a pan with the rue and pepper. Bring to the boil and simmer to reduce slightly. To serve, strain the barley and figs from the reserved cooking liquor and arrange them around the meat on a large serving plate. Break the sweet wine cakes in half and, on another plate, pour half the sauce over them. Pour the rest of the sauce over the meat, then arrange the cakes on the serving plate along with any sauce that they have not absorbed. Carve the meat at the table.

Stuffed Kidneys

Grilled kidneys are made as follows: They are cut down the middle to spread them out, and seasoned with ground pepper, pine kernels and very finely chopped coriander and ground fennel seed. Then the kidneys are closed up, sewn together, wrapped in caul, parboiled in oil and fish sauce, and then baked in a crock or on a grill.

Apicius 7, 8

This is another one of my favourite dishes, excellent as a first or main course. At a food tasting of mine one of the 'guinea-pigs', a conservative eater, actually thanked me for curing him of a lifelong hatred of kidneys!

SERVES FOUR

8 LAMB'S KIDNEYS

10 FENNEL SEEDS, ROASTED FOR 5 MINUTES IN A MODERATE OVEN

4 OZ (⅔ CUP/120 G) PINE KERNELS, SOAKED OVERNIGHT IN WHITE WINE

1 GENEROUS HANDFUL OF FRESH CORIANDER

1 LEVEL TEASPOON GROUND BLACK PEPPER

2 TABLESPOONS (30 ML) OLIVE OIL

2 TABLESPOONS (30 ML) FISH SAUCE

1 PIG'S CAUL (OPTIONAL)

Skin the kidneys, split in half and remove any fibres. In a mortar, pound the fennel seeds to a coarse powder. Strain the pine kernels and add them to the mortar with the coriander. Continue to pound the mixture until it is of a uniform texture. Add the pepper. Place a spoonful of the mixture in the centre of each kidney and close them up. If you can obtain pig's caul from a butcher, use it to wrap each kidney to prevent the stuffing from coming out. Otherwise sew up with a little cotton thread or secure with a cocktail stick. Combine the oil and fish sauce in a frying-pan and heat. Seal the kidneys for 2 minutes on each side, then transfer them and the sauce to a small baking dish and finish in a pre-heated oven at 350°F (180°C/gas mark 4) for a further 10 minutes. Serve as a first course or as a light snack.

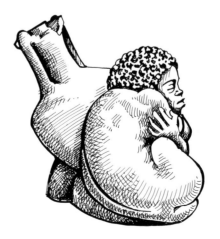

A child slave asleep in the wine cellar: terracotta from south Italy, about 320 BC.

Honeyed Mushrooms

Place the chopped stalks in a new baking-dish, adding pepper, lovage and
a little honey. Blend with fish sauce and, sparingly, oil.
Apicius 7, 13, 6

SERVES FOUR

1 TABLESPOON (15 ML) OLIVE OIL

1 TABLESPOON (15 ML) FISH SAUCE

1 TABLESPOON (30 G) HONEY

2 TEASPOONS CHOPPED FRESH LOVAGE OR CELERY LEAF

½ TEASPOON GROUND BLACK PEPPER

8 OZ (225 G) LARGE OPEN MUSHROOMS, THICKLY SLICED

Combine the oil, fish sauce and honey in a pan and bring to the boil. Add the lovage and pepper and the sliced mushrooms. Cook out briskly in order to reduce the liquids so that, when you serve, the fish sauce and natural water will have been boiled away and the honey and oil give a glaze to the mushrooms.

These mushrooms are easily prepared as an accompaniment to many of the main course dishes in the book.

Mushrooms were a prized delicacy in ancient times – but there were dangers involved in eating them. Not everybody knew how to distinguish the poisonous kinds from those that were good to eat. Greek and Roman medical writers therefore suggest many antidotes to mushroom poisoning: illogically, to us, these antidotes often included the ingredients with which mushrooms were cooked. Perhaps the danger was part of the pleasure for the dedicated gourmet, as with the Japanese taste for poisonous sushi. The Roman emperor Claudius (10 BC–AD 54), who began the conquest of Britain (see chapter 7), died in agony after tucking into a dish of *boleti*, but this, everyone said, was not the fault of the mushrooms: his wife had added poison to the dish.

The ancient recipe given above is also for *boleti*. These were not necessarily the kind that is now called boletus (*cèpe*); they were more probably *Agaricus caesarius*, close to our common champignon mushrooms. In any case they were evidently regarded as a delicacy, since the trouble was taken to serve the stalks separately. I find that large open mushrooms are best for this recipe, though you can certainly use dried *cèpes*.

7

ON HADRIAN'S WALL

Rome's world empire stretched from the banks of the Euphrates to the western shores of Lusitania (Portugal), from the Libyan desert to the marshy banks of the lower Rhine. The Roman army had conquered most of this huge territory, and the army was now the empire's guarantee against unrest and invasion. An army of something like half a million men was a miracle of organisation. The infrastructure that supported it had a great influence on life throughout the Roman provinces, an influence that in many ways can still be traced.

Paved Roman roads arrowed from capital to provincial town and onwards to the frontier fortresses. Many routes were studded with official staging posts: at first no more than inns where messengers could change horses, these often grew into centres of local trade. Standard army rations, and standard officers' luxuries, travelled hundreds of miles, by cart and river barge, to reach distant units. Taxes were dispatched inwards, army pay and retirement bonuses were sent outwards, swelling a monetary economy: at last a standard maximum price, empire-wide, could be fixed for all the necessities of army life.

There were few inns in classical Greece, if Greek texts are anything to go by. By contrast, inns are part of the story of Roman life. The inns of Italy come to life in a narrative sketch by the poet Horace (65–8 BC): 'We made straight for Benevento, where an attentive host almost burnt his inn down while spit-roasting some lean thrushes for us! A stray spark from dying embers in his old kitchen flew up and set the ceiling alight. Hungry guests and nervous slaves were in competition, rescuing the dinner and putting out the fire.'

Then there is a scrap of conversation, found by archaeologists where it was written as an advertisement on an inn wall to catch the traveller's eye:

'Innkeeper, how much do I owe you?'
'There was the wine, twopence halfpenny; bread, a penny; relish, twopence.'
'That's right.'
'The girl, eightpence.'
'Right.'
'Hay for your mule, twopence.'
'That mule will be the ruin of me.'

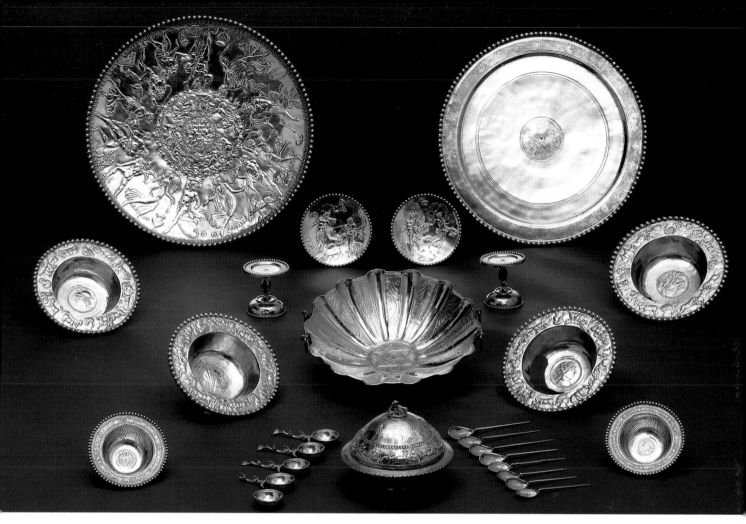

The first attempt to incorporate distant Britain among Rome's provinces was made by Julius Caesar. His two raids, in 55 and 54 BC, achieved nothing. The fourth emperor, Claudius, however, succeeded where Caesar had failed. The emperor himself spent only a fortnight in the cold wet province, but the invasion he ordered in AD 43 had resulted, within sixty years, in the conquest of all of south Britain as far as the Solway Firth and the River Tyne. Indeed, Roman troops penetrated at times far into Scotland.

Three or sometimes four Roman legions were stationed here. Far from the traditional wine-producing districts of Europe, Romans in Britain demanded wine to drink, lentils to eat, walnuts, figs and olives to chew. All these were imported, and experiments were certainly made with planting vines and walnuts. Roman soldiers and civilians expected familiar flavours in their food, the celery and carrot, the fennel and

Fine Roman silverware from the Mildenhall Treasure, found in Suffolk in the 1940s, probably buried about AD 360. Reliefs show satyrs and maenads, attendants of Bacchus; there are also Christian motifs on some pieces.

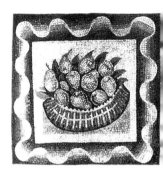

coriander, the pears, peaches and mulberries of the warm south. Their demands have made a lasting difference to the food and drink of Britain, for all these and many other fruits, vegetables and herbs were introduced to the island in Roman times and in most cases have grown here ever since.

We know this from archaeology, not from literature. The Romans wrote very little that survives about their most northerly province. But writings of Romans in Britain have in the last few years come quite unexpectedly to light. At one of the forts on the northern border – Vindolanda, in the remote valley of the south Tyne, close to where Hadrian's Wall would soon be built – a collection of letters, official and private, written in ink on thin sheets of alder wood and discarded around AD 100, has been excavated and painstakingly deciphered. One is an invitation to a lady's birthday party (see page 118). Another seems to be a day-book recording food supplies issued to soldiers: 'June 24. Barley, 12 gallons; beer, 6 gallons; wine, 3½ gallons; vinegar, 2 pints; *muria*, 1½ pints; pork fat, 15 pints.' The influence, then, was not all one way: somebody at Vindolanda required twice as much beer, the strange malted brew of Gaul and Britain, as traditional wine!

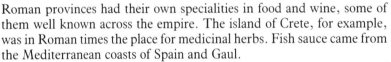

Roman provinces had their own specialities in food and wine, some of them well known across the empire. The island of Crete, for example, was in Roman times the place for medicinal herbs. Fish sauce came from the Mediterranean coasts of Spain and Gaul.

The wines of Greece and Italy were both famous, but the wines of Gaul, the Rhineland and Spain were beginning to develop a reputation. Pliny surveys the wines of Narbonensis (Provence and Languedoc), describing what are evidently ancestors to the aperitifs of today: 'Between Pyrenees and Alps is Marseille, with wine of two styles: one of them, called "sappy", is made particularly rich for mixing with others. The reputation of Béziers is confined to Gaul. On the other wines of Narbonensis I will say nothing: they have set up a factory to produce them, altering the flavour with smoke, and (I wish it were not so) with herbs and noxious drugs. One merchant even falsifies the flavour and colour with aloes.'

With a menu based on this chapter, good traditional-style French or Spanish wines will go very well. The fortified wines of the Mediterranean shores – Malaga, Maury, Rivesaltes – probably preserve something of the ancient style (though Romans did not literally fortify their wines). There are long-established dessert white wines from here too, Valencia, Muscat de Frontignan and others.

Soft-boiled Eggs

For soft-boiled eggs: pepper, lovage, steeped pine kernels. Moisten with
honey, vinegar, blend with fish sauce.
Apicius 7, 17, 3

SERVES FOUR

4 OZ (⅔ CUP/120 G) PINE KERNELS, SOAKED OVERNIGHT
IN A LITTLE WHITE WINE

1 TEASPOON CHOPPED FRESH LOVAGE OR CELERY LEAF

1 TABLESPOON (15 ML) FISH SAUCE

1 TABLESPOON (30 G) HONEY

1 TABLESPOON (15 ML) WHITE WINE VINEGAR

½ TEASPOON GROUND BLACK PEPPER

4 EGGS, SOFT-BOILED

Strain the pine kernels and pound or process them to a smooth paste. Add the lovage, fish sauce, honey, vinegar and pepper and continue to pound or process until you have a smooth mixture – at least, I usually serve it very smooth, but it is just as good if the texture remains rather crunchy. Finish the dish as if you were making egg mayonnaise and garnish with cucumber, dressed as in the following recipe.

As an aside, here is another example of how ancient cuisine has to be reconstructed from a jigsaw puzzle of evidence. How did classical Greek cooks slice eggs? How were sorbs, the southern European relatives of the rowan berry, made edible? The story of the origin of love, told at Plato's *Symposium* (chapter 2), happens to give the answer to both questions: 'At that,' Aristophanes said, 'the Creator proceeded to cut the spherical beings in half, just like someone cutting sorbs in half ready for pickling, or slicing eggs with hairs.'

Cucumber Dressing

Cucumber: pepper, pennyroyal, honey or raisin wine, fish sauce and vinegar. Sometimes also asafoetida.

Apicius 3, 6, 3

SERVES SIX

½ CUCUMBER, PEELED AND THINLY SLICED
I TEASPOON CHOPPED FRESH OR DRIED PENNYROYAL (OR MINT)
2 TABLESPOONS (30 ML) RAISIN WINE
I TABLESPOON (15 ML) FISH SAUCE
I TABLESPOON (15 ML) RED WINE VINEGAR
2 DROPS ASAFOETIDA TINCTURE OR I PINCH ASAFOETIDA POWDER

Arrange the cucumber in a dish; combine the other ingredients and pour over. Cover the dish with plastic wrap and refrigerate for a couple of hours to marinate.

The birthday invitation found at Vindolanda. Letter of about AD 100 from Claudia Severa to Lepidina, wife of the commander Cerialis. 'On 11 September, sister, when I celebrate my birthday, I invite you warmly to come to us: you will make the day more enjoyable for me if you are here. My greetings to your Cerialis. Aelius and the little boy send theirs.' The letter was written by a servant, but Severa adds in her own hand: 'I'm expecting you, sister. Keep well, dear heart, as I hope I will too; goodbye.'

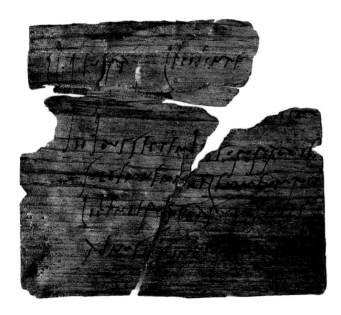
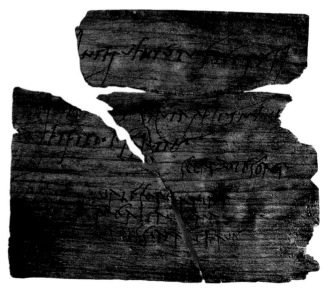

White Sausages

Sausages: husk grains of emmer, boil together with the liquid in which intestines have cooked and with finely-chopped white of leek. When boiled, remove from the heat. Mince fat and bits of meat and mix all together. Crush pepper, lovage, 3 eggs; mix all this, in the mortar, with pine kernels and whole peppercorns. Moisten with fish sauce. Stuff intestines. Boil and grill briefly or just boil: serve.

Apicius 2, 5, 3

SERVES SIX

1 LEEK (WHITE PART ONLY), FINELY CHOPPED

2 TABLESPOONS (30 G) CRACKED WHEAT

12 OZ (340 G) MINCED (GROUND) BELLY PORK

2 TEASPOONS CHOPPED FRESH LOVAGE OR CELERY LEAF

2 EGGS

2 TABLESPOONS (30 G) PINE KERNELS

2 TABLESPOONS (30 ML) FISH SAUCE

1 TEASPOON BLACK PEPPERCORNS

½ TEASPOON GROUND BLACK PEPPER

SAUSAGE SKINS

Put 5 fl oz (⅔ cup/150 ml) water in a pan with the finely chopped white of leek. Bring to the boil and simmer briefly. Sprinkle the cracked wheat into the water and cook out for 5 minutes. Strain and turn out into a bowl and allow to cool. Combine all the ingredients in a food processor and mix well. Stuff the sausages (for advice see Smoked Sausages on page 90) and twist the individual lengths into a spiral. Place the sausages in a pan of cold water, bring it slowly to the boil and simmer for 20 minutes. They will at this stage be white and can be eaten either hot or cold. If you wish, you can grill (broil) them briefly to give them colour.

White sausages were traditionally served with a grain or pulse (legume) pottage. I find the recipe for Vitellian Peas, which follows, excellent as an accompaniment.

Vitellian Peas

Vitellian peas (or broad (fava) beans). Boil and stir the peas till smooth.
Crush pepper, lovage, ginger, and to the seasonings add hard-boiled yolks
of egg, 3 oz honey, fish sauce, wine and vinegar. Put all this in a saucepan
with the crushed seasonings. Add oil and leave to boil. Add to the peas,
and stir again if still firm. Add honey and serve.
Apicius 5, 3, 5

SERVES FOUR

8 OZ (225 G) MARROWFAT OR OTHER DRIED PEAS OR
I LB (450 G) FRESH BROAD (FAVA) BEANS

¾ IN (2 CM) FRESH ROOT GINGER

2 TEASPOONS CHOPPED FRESH LOVAGE OR CELERY LEAF

½ TEASPOON GROUND BLACK PEPPER

3 COOKED EGG YOLKS

3 TABLESPOONS (90 G) CLEAR HONEY

2 TABLESPOONS (30 ML) FISH SAUCE

5 FL OZ (⅔ CUP/150 ML) WHITE WINE

3 FL OZ (⅓ CUP/80 ML) WHITE WINE VINEGAR

I TABLESPOON (15 ML) OLIVE OIL

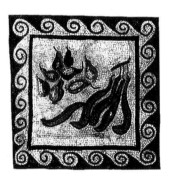

Soak the peas overnight in cold water. The next day strain, place in a pan and cover with fresh cold water. Bring to the boil and simmer for 1–1½ hours until tender, adding extra boiling water if necessary. When cooked, drain and beat until smooth. Alternatively, allow to cool, then blend in a food processor. Leave to one side. If using broad beans, cook them in boiling salted water for 4–6 minutes or until tender, then drain and purée.

You will need a pestle and mortar to make the sauce. Peel and chop the ginger and pound with the lovage and pepper. Add the cooked egg yolks and continue pounding until you have a smooth paste. Add the honey and fish sauce and stir till smooth. Flush out the mortar with the wine and vinegar and transfer to a saucepan. Add the oil, bring to the boil and simmer gently for a few minutes. Add the contents of the saucepan to the peas (or beans) and reheat. I find the peas now sweet enough, so I omit the final addition of honey given in the original recipe.

Pork with Apple

Minutal Matianum. Put oil, fish sauce and stock into a saucepan: chop leek, coriander, small meatballs. Dice a cooked shoulder of pork (with the crackling left on). Cook all together. Half way through cooking, add cored diced Matian apples. While cooking, pound together pepper, cumin, fresh coriander or coriander seed, mint, asafoetida root; pour on vinegar, honey, fish sauce, a little concentrated must, and some of the cooking liquor: adjust the flavour with a little vinegar. Bring to the boil. When it boils crumble pastry to bind the sauce. Sprinkle pepper and serve.

Apicius 4, 3, 4

SERVES FOUR

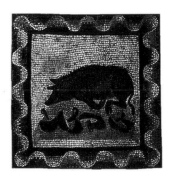

I LB (450 G) BONED LEAN PORK

3 TABLESPOONS (90 G) CLEAR HONEY

I BAY LEAF

5 PEPPERCORNS

I CELERY STALK

8 OZ (225 G) MINCED (GROUND) BEEF

I SMALL EGG, BEATEN

I LARGE LEEK

I LARGE HANDFUL OF FRESH CORIANDER

I LB (450 G) SMALL SWEET APPLES

10 FL OZ (1¼ CUPS/280 ML) WHITE WINE

5 FL OZ (⅔ CUP/150 ML) WHITE WINE VINEGAR

2 TABLESPOONS (30 ML) OLIVE OIL

5 FL OZ (⅔ CUP/150 ML) FISH SAUCE

2 TEASPOONS GROUND CUMIN

2 TEASPOONS GROUND CORIANDER

I TEASPOON ASAFOETIDA POWDER OR
5 DROPS ASAFOETIDA TINCTURE

2 TEASPOONS CHOPPED FRESH OR 1½ TEASPOONS DRIED MINT

CORNFLOUR (CORNSTARCH) TO THICKEN

FRESHLY GROUND BLACK PEPPER

Place the pork in a pan of water with 1 tablespoon (30 g) honey, the bay leaf, peppercorns and celery stalk. Bring to the boil and simmer for 1 hour. Leave to cool in the water. Form the beef into small balls with a little beaten egg to bind them.

Slice the leek, chop the fresh coriander and peel, core and segment the apples. In a large saucepan put the wine, 10 fl oz (1¼ cups/280 ml) cooking liquor from the pork, the vinegar, oil, fish sauce and the remaining 2 tablespoons (60 g) honey. Dice the pork and add this to the pot with the meatballs. Bring to the boil and add the leek, coriander and slices of apple. Simmer for about 30 minutes until the meat is fully cooked. Add the cumin, ground coriander, asafoetida and mint when almost cooked and thicken with a little cornflour. Finish with a generous seasoning of black pepper.

The Chaourse Treasure, probably a wealthy family's complete silver service, buried in Roman Gaul about AD 260.

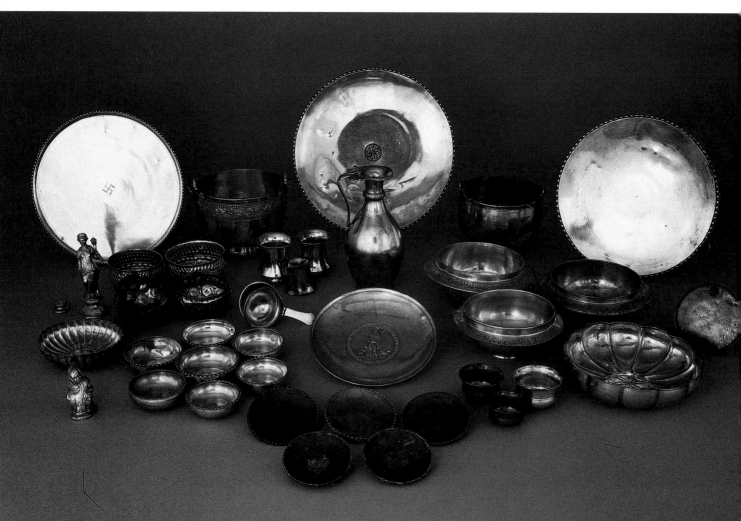

Did the Latin name for this dish come from Gaius Matius, friend of the Emperor Augustus, because it was invented in his kitchen or described in his household book? Or did it come from a fine variety of apples, developed by Matius and called 'Matian' after him? These apples grew best around a certain village in northern Italy on the southern foothills of the Alps of Veneto.

Pork and apple have traditionally been served together in Britain for centuries: this is a fitting recipe for us to revive. The herbs and spices were all available in Roman Britain, whether grown here or imported. Even the fish sauce, *garum*, was made in Britain: an archaeological site near London is unmistakably a Roman *garum* factory.

Stuffed Chicken

Stuffed chicken. Draw the chicken from the neck. Crush pepper, lovage, ginger, chopped meat, boiled emmer; crush boiled brain, break eggs in and work into a smooth mixture. Blend with fish sauce and add a little oil, whole peppercorns, plenty of pine kernels. Make up into a stuffing and stuff the chicken (or sucking-pig), so that a little room is left. You can do the same with a capon. Cook, discarding the bones.

Apicius 6, 9, 14

SERVES FOUR

I IN (2.5 CM) FRESH ROOT GINGER

12 OZ (340 G) MINCED (GROUND) BEEF, OR 6 OZ (170 G) MINCED
(GROUND) BEEF AND 6 OZ (170 G) COOKED LAMB'S BRAINS

6 OZ (170 G) CRACKED WHEAT, COOKED FOR 20 MINUTES AND DRAINED

2 TEASPOONS CHOPPED FRESH LOVAGE OR CELERY LEAF

I LEVEL TEASPOON GROUND BLACK PEPPER

I TABLESPOON (15 ML) OLIVE OIL

4 TABLESPOONS (60 G) PINE KERNELS

2 FL OZ (¼ CUP/60 ML) FISH SAUCE

I TEASPOON BLACK PEPPERCORNS

2 EGGS

I FRESH CHICKEN, WEIGHING ABOUT 2 LB (900 G)

Peel and chop the ginger. Place the cooked brains and/or minced beef in a food processor along with the cracked wheat, and all the other spices, herbs and liquids. Mix well; add the eggs and process again. If you are using a boned chicken, spread out the skin on a chopping board, arranging the leg and wing pieces in their correct place. Spread the mixture over the breast area and also into the leg and wing cavities. Bring the skin over the stuffing and fold the edges in at each end. Turn the chicken over and rearrange the skin in a chicken shape. Secure the skin flap with a couple of stitches of kitchen string. If you are using a whole chicken, simply stuff the cavity in the normal way. At this stage you can either roast the bird with a little olive oil and salt and pepper; or, if you have a boned bird, you can boil it, as a galantine is normally cooked. Wrap the galantine in muslin to hold its shape and cook for 1½ hours in water to which you have added a bay leaf and a stick of celery.

There is no sauce for this dish, which is very unusual for a recipe from *Apicius*. Follow the recipe for the sauce that accompanies Stuffed Gourd on page 105 if you would like to serve it with a sauce.

It is not clear in the ancient recipe whether only a capon would be boned before stuffing, or whether that applies to chicken as well. The intricacies of completely boning a chicken may not be to your taste: you can ask your butcher to do it for you (or follow the instructions in a good cookery book such as Mrs Beeton's) or you can treat this simply as a recipe for chicken with stuffing and omit the boning altogether – it will be a great success either way.

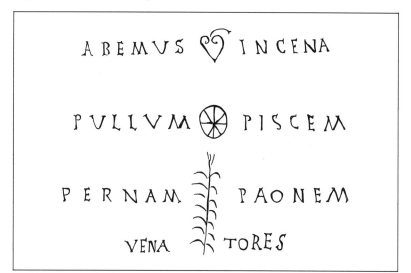

Inscription from a Roman inn, giving its permanent menu: 'Huntsmen, we have for dinner chicken, fish, ham, peacock.'

Patina of Pears

Patina *of pears. Boil and core pears, crush with pepper, cumin, honey, raisin wine, fish sauce and a little oil. Add eggs to make the* patina, *season with pepper, and serve.*

Apicius 4, 2, 35

SERVES FOUR

1½ LB (675 G) FIRM PEARS

10 FL OZ (1¼ CUPS/280 ML) RAISIN WINE

2 TABLESPOONS (60 G) CLEAR HONEY

1 TEASPOON GROUND CUMIN

1 TABLESPOON (15 ML) OLIVE OIL

1 TABLESPOON (15 ML) FISH SAUCE

3 EGGS

½ TEASPOON GROUND BLACK PEPPER

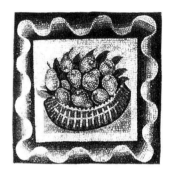

Peel and core the pears and chop them roughly. Cook them till soft in the raisin wine and honey. Pass the whole mixture through a sieve or process it till smooth. Add the cumin, oil, fish sauce and eggs and process again till smooth. Pour into a greased casserole dish and bake in a pre-heated oven at 375°F (190°C/gas mark 5) for 20 minutes or until it sets. Serve warm with a sprinkling of freshly ground black pepper.

A *patina*, in Roman cuisine, is a dish that is either set with eggs or includes eggs as an ingredient. It could be sweet or savoury, and the appearance could vary just as much as the flavour. It was originally named after the typical serving dish, a *patina* or *patella*.

This first *patina* (there are more in chapter 8) is a fruit-based egg custard flavoured with cumin. An odd combination, you may think, but it works very well and has been one of my more popular dishes at dinner-parties.

8

SUPPER AT THE BATHS

The big city, too, had its cookshops, its bars and its taverns. Juvenal made fun of the old men who still frequented the all-night bars at Rome's harbour town, Ostia, as if they were youngsters:

The Phoenician host, greasy with respectful hair-oil, runs to welcome his guest's approach and calls him 'Master!', why not 'King!' Here's the waitress running to him with her skirt hitched up, already uncorking a bottle. Send to Ostia for him, Caesar, look in the big tavern there: you'll find him lying alongside some brawler, in among sailors and thieves and runaways, with hangmen and coffin-makers and a sodden priest of Cybele, his cymbals strangely silent. In the tavern all are equally free, all drink from a common cup, the couch is barred to no man, the table is no closer to one than it is to another.

We begin to sense the reality of ancient city life as we read a letter by the philosopher Seneca (c. AD 4–65), complaining of what he had to listen to just outside his apartment window: 'pancake-sellers and a sausage-vendor and a confectioner and all the proprietors of restaurants, selling their wares with miscellaneous shouts, each in his distinctive accent'.

What was the daily routine of those who lived in imperial Rome? Romans tended to eat little during the first part of the day: a breakfast, *ientaculum*, was a snack that many did not trouble to take at all, and only the greedy wanted a big lunch, *prandium*. Workers no doubt found a lunch in a tavern or cookshop. Those who survived through patronage (as did many in Rome) attended on some rich or powerful figure, no doubt hoping that there would be something for themselves when he paused for a bite to eat.

The late afternoon and evening were the time for relaxation. There was no better preparation for a big evening meal, the one big meal of the day, than a couple of hours at the baths. It was a favourite occupation that was well provided for. Grand public and smaller private baths clustered all over Rome, fashionable meeting places, ideal locations for informal business discussions. The ritual was itself soothing, the sequence of exercise, steam bath, warm bath, cold bath.

Encolpius of the *Satyricon* first caught sight of his future host, Trimalchio, in the exercise room at the baths, where the great man was

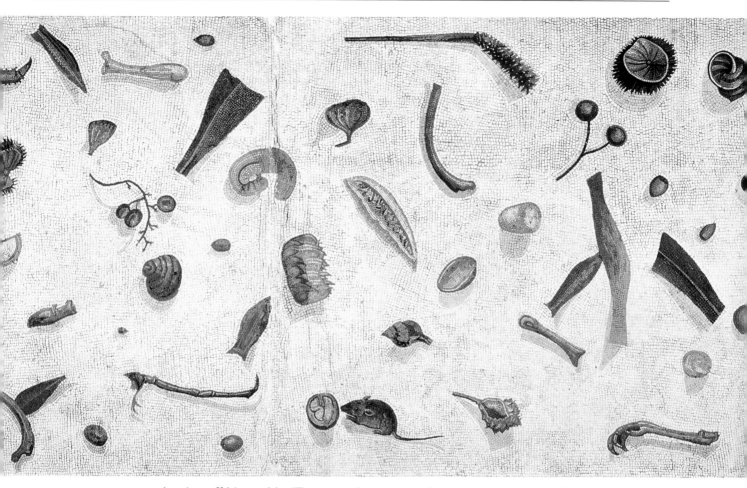

showing off his wealth: 'Two eunuchs were standing about among the ball-players, one of them holding a silver chamber-pot. Trimalchio snapped his fingers, and the eunuch held out the pot as his master went on playing. After emptying his bladder Trimalchio called for water for his hands, and rinsed his fingers, drying them in a slave-boy's hair.'

The last of our vignettes of the ancient world presents a less ostentatious scene, a conversation at the Baths of Tigellinus (donated to the city of Rome, apparently, by Nero's fearsome minister). As we shall see, attached to the baths were bars and restaurants: a party could easily spend a whole evening there. The extract is taken from an unusual manuscript, a bilingual phrase-book, *Daily Conversation*, originally intended for Greeks learning Latin and Romans learning Greek.

Mosaic from Roman Italy. Fishbones, crab claws, fruit stones, snail shells . . . the remains of a banquet, permanently depicted on a dining-room floor.

The imaginary speaker is heading a party of friends. Unlike Trimalchio he has no slaves of his own, but he has come to the baths for an evening of enjoyment and he begins by choosing an attendant: 'Follow us. Yes, you. Look after our things carefully, and find us a place. I'll just speak to the perfumier – hello, Julius, give me incense and myrrh for twenty. No, no, best quality. Now, boy, undo my shoes. Take my clothes. Oil me. All right, let's go in.'

After exercise and bathing the friends move on to the restaurant. A party as large as twenty can order a wide variety of starters and main courses (and the author of the phrase book works in as many variations as he can):

'A good bath, sir?'

'This is my party. Mix wine for us and let's recline. For starters give us beetroot or gourd: add some fish sauce to that. Give us radishes, and a knife: and some lettuce and cucumber, with vinegar and fish sauce dressing. Bring us a trotter, a black pudding and a sow's womb. We'll all have white bread. The sauce wants more oil in it. Scale the pilchards before you put them on the table. We'll have pork shoulder and ham and some mustard. Isn't the fish grilled yet?

'Now, then, some slices of venison, wild boar, chicken, hare. Give everybody a portion of cabbage. Slice the boiled meat. Now serve the drinks.

'We've all had a drink. Bring the turtle-doves and the pheasant: bring the udder, and add some *alec*. Let's eat: it's just right. Give us the roast sucking-pig. That's very hot. You'd better carve it. Bring honey in a jug. Bring a fatted goose, and some pickles.

'Take round some water to rinse people's hands. Bring us yoghurt, if you have any, with honey, and some halva. Cut it into slices and we can share it out.

'That was a good meal. Give the waiters and the servants something to eat and drink, and also the cook, because he has served us well. Come on, let's go out for a walk . . .'

The recipes that follow, like many of those in earlier chapters, are taken from the Roman cookery book *Apicius*. This unique compilation is believed to date from the very end of the Roman Empire, perhaps about AD 400. Dating such a text is a very difficult matter. Apicius was the name of a legendary gourmet of four hundred years earlier, under Augustus: the book we know is clearly named after him, but is any of it actually his? The 'works of Apicius' were a bedside book, it is said, for a rich dilettante in AD 120: did he fall asleep over the *Apicius* that we know? Probably not. Although it demands many expensive ingredients, *Apicius* as we know it is a severely practical book. It is written in lower-class Latin, 'vulgar Latin', not for rich men to read in bed but for cooks to use.

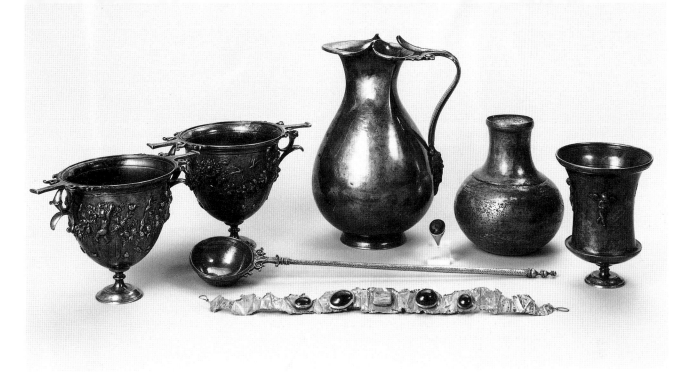

Finally we may wonder what wines were served at the baths of Tigellinus and to accompany the recipes of *Apicius*. The history of wine in later Rome has still to be written, but it seems that although much wine was imported from Spain, Gaul and Greece, Italians remained proud of their own vintages.

All through the empire no author dared to say in so many words that Italian wines were better than Greek. The western Roman Empire fell. The last emperor, Romulus Augustulus, was deposed in AD 476. The Italian statesman Cassiodorus, minister to a Gothic king, was at last bold enough (in a letter to his agent, written about AD 500) to speak the truth: 'The Count of the Patrimony reports that the royal wine cellars are almost bare of *Acinaticum*. Go to the estate-owners of Verona and offer them a price that they will hasten to accept. It is a wine of which Italy may be proud. Clever Greece may boast its various products, its wines mixed with spices or flavoured with sea water, but in all its elaborations it has nothing like this.'

Verona is 'Italy's most active wine centre' according to Burton Anderson's *Wine Atlas of Italy*. Nowadays its wines range from the dry white Soave and dry red Valpolicella to the headier Recioto (a sweet red *passito* made from sun-dried grapes) and Amarone of Valpolicella. The last is a most unusual wine: a red from sun-dried grapes which is powerful, dry, even slightly bitter. Perhaps this venerable wine retains something of the style that so impressed Cassiodorus.

Roman silverware which was buried, alongside a rare coin of Mark Antony, in the grave of some unknown admirer of the maverick Roman statesman of the 1st century BC.

Seafood Rissoles with a Cumin Sauce

Seafood rissoles are made with cigales and lobsters, with cuttlefish, with squid, with langoustes. You flavour the rissole with pepper, fish sauce, cumin, asafoetida root.
Apicius 2, 1

Cumin sauce for oysters and shellfish: pepper, lovage, parsley, dried mint, fairly generous cumin, honey, vinegar, fish sauce.
Apicius 1, 29 [1, 15, 2]

These rissoles are delicious made with Pacific prawns, scampi, or fresh lobster meat and crawfish tails, all of which are available frozen from any fishmonger. The rissoles are apparently made without any binding ingredient, such as egg. They tend to break up when cooked in the sauce: that is why I add a little egg to hold them together and (as you will probably be using frozen shellfish) a small quantity of breadcrumbs to soak up the excess fluid. The rissoles are ideal as a first course or as a light lunch.

SERVES FOUR

8 OZ (225 G) PACIFIC PRAWNS, SCAMPI OR LOBSTER MEAT
(OTHER SEAFOOD CAN BE SUBSTITUTED)

½ TEASPOON ASAFOETIDA POWDER OR
4 DROPS ASAFOETIDA TINCTURE

½ TEASPOON GROUND BLACK PEPPER

I LEVEL TEASPOON GROUND CUMIN

I EGG

2 TABLESPOONS (30 ML) FISH SAUCE

I TABLESPOON (10 G) BREADCRUMBS

FLOUR FOR DUSTING

Sauce

5 FL OZ (⅔ CUP/150 ML) WHITE WINE VINEGAR

5 FL OZ (⅔ CUP/150 ML) WHITE WINE

2 TABLESPOONS (60 G) CLEAR HONEY

2 TABLESPOONS (30 ML) FISH SAUCE

1 LEVEL TEASPOON GROUND CUMIN

1 BAY LEAF

1 TEASPOON CHOPPED FRESH OR ½ TEASPOON DRIED MINT

1 HANDFUL OF FRESH PARSLEY, CHOPPED

1 TEASPOON CHOPPED FRESH LOVAGE OR CELERY LEAF

GROUND BLACK PEPPER

Defrost the shellfish thoroughly, drain and pat dry well with kitchen paper. Pound it down in a mortar or process it to a coarse mince. Add the asafoetida, pepper, cumin, egg, fish sauce and breadcrumbs and mix well. Turn out on to a floured board and form into about 12 balls. Roll in extra flour and leave to chill in the refrigerator while you prepare the sauce.

Combine the sauce ingredients in a frying-pan, bring to the boil and simmer briefly. Add the rissoles and poach them gently for about 10 minutes, turning them occasionally. Serve immediately, accompanied by the sauce.

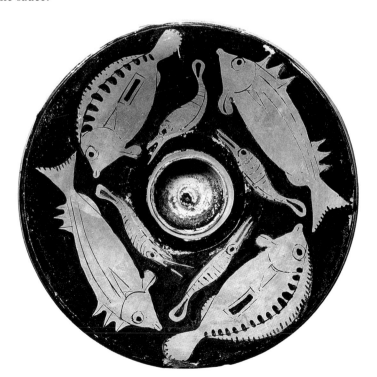

Two sea perch, two bass and four prawns, sketched on a 4th-century-BC 'fish-plate' from southern Italy.

Patina of Sole

Patina zomoteganon. Arrange any chosen fish, uncooked, in a pan. Add oil, fish sauce, wine, a bouquet of leek and coriander. While it cooks crush pepper, rub in a bouquet of lovage and oregano, add the juices from the cooked fish, beat in raw eggs, blend. Empty into the pan, allow to bind. When set, season with pepper and serve.

Apicius 4, 2, 27

This simple dish can be made with any fish of your choice. I find it particularly good with white fish such as sole or plaice.

SERVES TWO

2 FILLETS OF SOLE

I TABLESPOON (I5 ML) OLIVE OIL

2 TABLESPOONS (30 ML) FISH SAUCE

5 FL OZ (⅔ CUP/I50 ML) WHITE WINE

I BOUQUET GARNI OF LEEK AND FRESH CORIANDER

½ TEASPOON GROUND BLACK PEPPER

I TEASPOON CHOPPED FRESH LOVAGE OR CELERY LEAF

I TEASPOON CHOPPED FRESH OREGANO

2 EGGS

Place the fillets in a baking dish and pour on the oil, fish sauce and wine. Add the bouquet garni and bake in a pre-heated oven at 375°F (190°C/gas mark 5) for 15 minutes. Remove; drain off the cooking liquor and reserve. In a mortar pound the pepper, lovage, oregano and the cooked bouquet. Flush out the mixture with the cooking liquor and mix in the eggs. Pour this over the fish and return to the oven until it has set. Serve immediately sprinkled with freshly ground black pepper.

Roast Duck with Hazelnuts

Alternative sauce for birds: pepper, parsley, lovage, dried mint, safflower, moisten with wine, add roasted hazelnuts or almonds, a little honey, blend with wine and vinegar and fish sauce. Add oil to this mixture in the saucepan, heat, stir with fresh celery and calamint. Make incisions [in the birds] and pour the sauce over them.

Apicius 6, 5, 2

In this dish a mixture half-way between a sauce and a nut crumb coats the meat and creates a wonderfully crunchy texture outside while remaining fluid underneath. The bird can be, as indicated, an open choice. The recipe has a modern Christmassy feel which can be enhanced by the use of a duck, goose or even a pheasant – but I use chicken with equal success.

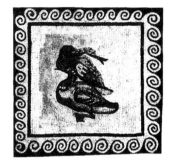

Two unusual herbs are called for in the ancient recipe. Safflower is often known as fake saffron: the powder sold today as 'saffron' is more than likely adulterated with safflower. Under its real name safflower is best known to us as a recently developed cooking oil. Calamint, still used in southern Europe as a culinary herb, is hard to find elsewhere; the closely related catmint is rather commoner and it is this that I have used (the Latin name *Nepeta* may, it seems, be applied to either).

SERVES FOUR

6 OZ (1½ CUPS/170 G) HAZELNUTS

2 TEASPOONS CHOPPED FRESH OR 1½ TEASPOONS DRIED MINT

2 TEASPOONS CHOPPED FRESH LOVAGE OR CELERY LEAF

2 TEASPOONS CHOPPED FRESH PARSLEY

1 TEASPOON CHOPPED FRESH CATMINT OR CALAMINT
(IF NOT AVAILABLE, INCREASE THE MINT)

2 TABLESPOONS (60 G) CLEAR HONEY

10 FL OZ (1¼ CUPS/280 ML) RED WINE

2 TABLESPOONS (30 ML) OLIVE OIL

2 TABLESPOONS (30 ML) RED WINE VINEGAR

5 FL OZ (⅔ CUP/150 ML) FISH SAUCE

1 TEASPOON GROUND BLACK PEPPER

PINCH SAFFRON POWDER OR STRANDS

3 LB (1.5 KG) DUCK, CHICKEN OR OTHER BIRD

SALT

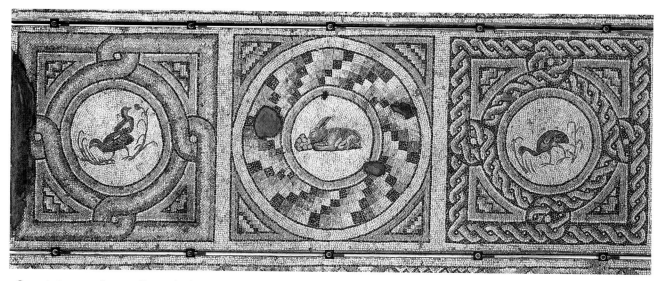

Game in its natural habitat, depicted on a mosaic from late Roman Syria. In the central vignette a hare feasts on grapes.

Roast the hazelnuts for 10 minutes in the oven at 350°F (180°C/gas mark 4). Pound or process them to a fine crumb. Add them to a saucepan with all the other ingredients for the sauce and bring slowly to the boil. Place the bird in a roasting pan and season well with salt and pepper. Cut into the breast and leg and open the incisions before pouring the sauce over the bird. Roast in the normal way in a pre-heated oven at 400°F (200°C/gas mark 6) for about 1½ hours. While cooking, repeatedly baste the bird to ensure that the skin is well covered in the nut mixture. As the wine reduces slightly the sauce will form a crust over the breast, which needs to be maintained once it has formed.

Patina of Asparagus

Alternative patina *of asparagus. Put asparagus tips in a mortar, pound, add wine, sieve. Pound pepper, lovage, fresh coriander, savory, onion, wine, fish sauce, oil. Put purée and spices in a greased shallow pan, and, if you wish, break eggs over it while cooking, so that it sets. Sprinkle ground pepper.*
Apicius 4, 2, 6

This is another savoury egg custard, typical of Roman cuisine, that deserves to be rediscovered. Roman gardeners and gourmets were the first to develop the thick-stemmed, delicately-flavoured asparagus with which we are familiar. But early Greeks, and the country people of the Roman Empire, already knew and appreciated *asparagi* – a group of wild plants, closely related to the cultivated variety, whose thinner, greener, young shoots are almost as succulent. Wild asparagus, if you can get it, would give an excellent flavour to this *patina*.

SERVES FOUR

2 BUNCHES ASPARAGUS OR 4 CANS GREEN ASPARAGUS TIPS

1 SMALL ONION, FINELY DICED

5 FL OZ (⅔ CUP/150 ML) WHITE WINE

1 TABLESPOON (15 ML) OLIVE OIL

2 TABLESPOONS (30 ML) FISH SAUCE

1 HANDFUL OF CHOPPED FRESH CORIANDER

1 TEASPOON CHOPPED FRESH OR DRIED SAVORY

1 TEASPOON CHOPPED FRESH LOVAGE OR CELERY LEAF

½ TEASPOON GROUND BLACK PEPPER

4 EGGS

Fresh asparagus must first be trimmed and steamed. Cut them down to about 6 in (15 cm) in length and peel the root end. Bind them into a bundle and stand them in a deep saucepan with boiling water half-way up the stalks. Cover with a lid and simmer for about 5–8 minutes until the root ends are tender, then refresh in cold water. Canned asparagus needs simply to be drained.

Now sauté the onion until tender and allow to cool. Place the asparagus and the onion in a food processor and purée; alternatively, pound them down to a smooth mixture. Add the wine, oil, fish sauce, coriander, savory, lovage and pepper. Pour the mixture into a greased shallow ovenproof dish and break the eggs on top. Bake in a pre-heated oven at 375°F (190°C/gas mark 5) for 10 minutes. Serve sprinkled with freshly ground black pepper.

Patina Apiciana

You make Patina Apiciana *as follows. Pieces of cooked womb, of fish, of chicken meat, warblers or cooked thrush breasts and whatever else is of top quality. Chop all this thoroughly, except the warblers. Mix raw eggs with oil. Crush pepper, lovage, moisten with fish sauce, wine, raisin wine, and set to warm in a saucepan, and bind with starch, after you have added all the chopped meats and let it come to the boil. When it is cooked, remove with its juices, with a spoon, and rearrange in a serving dish in layers, some with peppercorns, some with pine kernels. Place under each layer as a base a sheet of pasta, and put on each sheet one ladleful of the meat mixture. Finally pierce one sheet with a reed and place this one on top. Season with pepper. Before you put all these meats with the sauce into the saucepan you should have bound them with the eggs. The kind of bronze dish you need is shown below* [the illustration does not survive].

Apicius 4, 2, 14

SERVES SIX

10 FL OZ (1¼ CUPS/280 ML) WHITE WINE

10 FL OZ (1¼ CUPS/280 ML) RAISIN WINE

3 TABLESPOONS (45 ML) FISH SAUCE

2 TABLESPOONS (30 ML) OLIVE OIL,
PLUS A LITTLE EXTRA FOR BRUSHING

2 TEASPOONS CHOPPED FRESH LOVAGE OR CELERY LEAF

½ TEASPOON GROUND BLACK PEPPER

A LITTLE CORNFLOUR (CORNSTARCH)

4 OZ (120 G) COOKED, PEELED PRAWNS

4 OZ (120 G) COOKED CHICKEN BREAST

4 OZ (120 G) DICED SMOKED HAM

4 OZ (120 G) SMOKED SAUSAGE (SUCH AS THOSE ON PAGE 90), SLICED

4 TABLESPOONS (60 G) PINE KERNELS

1 TEASPOON BLACK PEPPERCORNS

2 EGGS

6–8 SHEETS OF PLAIN LASAGNE PASTA

Combine the wine, raisin wine, fish sauce, oil, lovage and ground pepper in a saucepan and bring to the boil. Thicken with a little cornflour and cook out briefly. Ensure that the prawns are defrosted and well drained, add them to the sauce with the meats and reheat. Add the pine kernels and peppercorns. Beat the eggs together and stir them into the mixture while off the heat. Slowly bring back to heat. Have ready your pasta sheets, cooked if necessary, and a greased baking dish. Beginning with a layer of meat, fill the dish with alternate layers of meat and lasagne in the normal way, finishing with a sheet of pasta. Brush this lightly with olive oil and cover with foil before reheating in a pre-heated oven at 400°F (200°C/gas mark 6) for 20 minutes.

This recipe is remarkably similar to lasagne in structure. The pasta sheets or *lagana*, a Greek term, are the same type as those used in the Layered Cheesecake (page 94), which were made from flour (or semolina) and water. I am in no doubt that this is the precursor of the traditional Italian lasagne. Durum wheat, now used for pasta, was already widely grown in the ancient world.

That wonderful phrase 'whatever else is of top quality', used in the original recipe, gives you free rein to choose your own filling. Don't be tied by my choice, though it was certainly acceptable to mix fish and meat together. Plain pasta sheets can be used or you can make your own by mixing a flour and water dough and rolling them out to the shape of the dish you use. Allow them to rest for an hour or so before assembling. We are not told to cook the dish again before serving, but I always bring it back to heat in the oven.

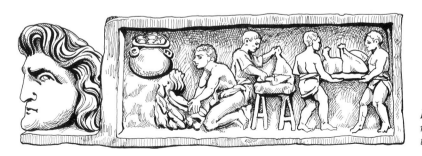

Kitchen work: Roman relief carving on a tomb, from Frascati.

Marrow or Squash Alexandria-style

Gourd Alexandrian fashion. Drain boiled gourd, season with salt, arrange in a dish. Crush pepper, cumin, coriander seed, fresh mint, asafoetida root. Moisten with vinegar. Add caryota *date, pine kernel; crush. Blend with honey, vinegar, fish sauce, concentrated must and oil, and pour the whole over the gourd. When it has boiled, season with pepper and serve.*

Apicius 3, 4, 3

SERVES SIX

I SMALL YOUNG MARROW OR YELLOW SQUASH

SALT

4 FRESH DATES, SOAKED IN A LITTLE WINE

2 TABLESPOONS (30 G) PINE KERNELS, SOAKED IN A LITTLE WINE

2 LEVEL TEASPOONS GROUND CUMIN

2 LEVEL TEASPOONS GROUND CORIANDER

½ TEASPOON GROUND BLACK PEPPER

2 TEASPOONS CHOPPED FRESH OR 1½ TEASPOONS DRIED MINT

½ TEASPOON ASAFOETIDA POWDER OR 5 DROPS ASAFOETIDA TINCTURE

2 TABLESPOONS (60 G) HONEY

I TABLESPOON (15 ML) DEFRUTUM (REDUCED RED GRAPE JUICE)

3 TABLESPOONS (45 ML) FISH SAUCE

2 TABLESPOONS (30 ML) OLIVE OIL

3 TABLESPOONS (45 ML) RED WINE VINEGAR

Slice the marrow or squash and steam or boil until *al dente* – still firm. Arrange the slices in a baking dish and sprinkle with a little salt.

You will need a pestle and mortar for the sauce. Take the stones from the dates and put the flesh in the mortar with the pine kernels. Mash them down to a paste. Transfer to a bowl and add the cumin, coriander, pepper, mint and asafoetida and mix well. Scrape down the mash and add the honey, defrutum, oil, fish sauce and vinegar. Stir into a smooth emulsion and pour over the marrow or squash. Cover with a lid or foil and reheat thoroughly in a pre-heated oven at 350°F (180°C/gas mark 4). Serve sprinkled with freshly ground pepper.

As in the recipe on page 105, we can substitute marrow or squash for the gourds that the Romans grew. This rich sauce complements their mild flavour very well.

Nut Omelette

Upside-down patina *as a sweet. Roast pine kernels and shelled broken nuts; crush with honey, pepper, fish sauce, milk, eggs, a little wine and oil, turn on to a round flat dish.*

Apicius 4, 2, 16

Serves Four

2 OZ (½ CUP/60 G) NIBBED ALMONDS

2 OZ (½ CUP/60 G) BROKEN WALNUTS OR HAZELNUTS

2 TABLESPOONS (30 G) PINE KERNELS

1 TABLESPOON (30 G) CLEAR HONEY

2 TABLESPOONS (60 ML) WHITE WINE

2 TABLESPOONS (60 ML) MILK

1 TABLESPOON (15 ML) FISH SAUCE OR SALT TO TASTE

6 EGGS

GROUND BLACK PEPPER

1 TABLESPOON (15 ML) OLIVE OIL

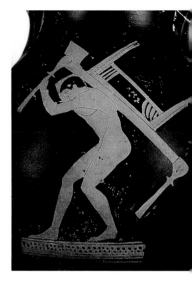

Vignette from a Greek vase. A slave clears up after the feast.

Combine all the nuts and roast them in the oven at 350°F (180°C/gas mark 4) for 10 minutes. Pound or grind them down to a uniform texture resembling coarse breadcrumbs. Place in a bowl and add the honey, wine, milk, fish sauce and the eggs and beat smooth. Season with plenty of black pepper. Heat the olive oil in a non-stick frying-pan and pour in the mixture. Cook as for a basic omelette and grill (broil) for 1 or 2 minutes to set the top. Cut into quarters and serve immediately.

No cooking instructions are given in the ancient text, but it is quite clear that this 'upside-down *patina*' is nothing less than a sweet omelette. The fish sauce is there to add the necessary touch of salt, and it can be replaced with salt.

A Note on Greek and Latin Sources
of Recipes

Some of these texts can be found in English translation: we give details of translations, and of the Greek and Latin texts we have used, in the guide to further reading that follows this note.

There were many Greek books about food. Almost the only ones that still survive to be read today are those written by physicians. Then, even more than now, a sensible diet was considered by many to be a guarantee of health. Fortunately the authors of diet books sometimes troubled to give the full list of ingredients for a recommended dish. Attached to recipes above, therefore, the names of Oribasius and Galen occur. Galen was a famous and successful Greek doctor who practised and lectured in Rome about AD 120. Oribasius lived in the fourth century AD; he was personal physician to the last pagan Roman emperor, Julian 'the Apostate' – and one of the main characters in Gore Vidal's historical novel *Julian*. Although we have not taken any recipes from it, a much earlier Greek text, known simply as *Regimen*, dating from about 400 BC, is full of fascinating information on the classical Greek diet. It is sometimes said to be the work of Hippocrates, the legendary founder of medical science. It can be read in English. At present the writings on food of Galen and Oribasius are not available in translation.

The true doyen of food writers is Archestratus, a Sicilian Greek of about 350 BC (see chapter 3). Archestratus' light poem *The Life of Luxury*, a sequence of lively rules on where to look for good fish and how to cook it, was already a rarity in ancient times and is now sadly lost forever; but a later scholar of food history, Athenaeus, an Egyptian Greek of about AD 200, quoted several extracts from the poem which we have been glad to use. There is now a complete English translation of the surviving bits of *The Life of Luxury*.

We have just mentioned Athenaeus' work. His *Deipnosophists*, a treasury of rare texts from earlier times, is also the source we used for recipes from other lost Greek food books. There is a complete English translation.

Gourmet cookery was probably taken to Rome by Greek cooks. Greeks who wrote cookery books in Rome included Chrysippus of Tyana and Paxamus, said by some to be the inventor of the biscuit (cookie). Their work is known only in scraps, by way of Athenaeus and a medieval Greek farming manual, *Geoponica*. Apart from these there are the recipes of Cato (see chapter 5) and other writers on farming.

The cookery of the later Roman Empire, uniting both Greek and Roman traditions, was codified in the one complete surviving cookery manuscript from the ancient world, the well-known *Apicius*. Those who want to see the full range of these recipes can find them easily (see below), because, in general, previously published books on Roman cookery have simply been adaptations of *Apicius*. Our aim in this book has been to give a wider view of Greek and Roman food.

Further Reading

Here are the texts on classical food that can be read in English translation. In this list, LCL means the Loeb Classical Library, which gives the original text parallel with an English translation. This useful series is kept permanently in print at a standard price per volume. It is published by Harvard University Press, Cambridge, Mass. (and used to be co-published by Heinemann, London).

Apicius. The best translation is *Apicius: the Roman Cookery Book* tr. B. Flower and E. Rosenbaum (London, 1961), but it is out of print. Still available is John Edwards, *The Roman Cookery of Apicius* (London, 1985).

ARCHESTRATUS. See *Archestratus: the Life of Luxury* tr. J. Wilkins and S. Hill (Totnes, 1994).

ATHENAEUS. See *Athenaeus: The Deipnosophists* tr. C. B. Gulick. 7 vols (LCL, 1927–41).

CATO. See *Marcus Porcius Cato on Agriculture; Marcus Terentius Varro on Agriculture* tr. W. D. Hooper and H. B. Ash (LCL, 1934).

HIPPOLOCHUS. See 'The Wedding Feast of Caranus the Macedonian' tr. A. Dalby in *Petits Propos Culinaires* no. 29 (1988), or vol. 2 of the LCL Athenaeus.

PETRONIUS. See *The Satyricon* tr. W. Arrowsmith (Ann Arbor, 1959), or tr. J. P. Sullivan (London, 1965).

PHILOXENUS. See 'The Banquet of Philoxenus' tr. A. Dalby in *Petits Propos Culinaires* no. 26 (1987).

PLINY. See *Pliny: Natural History* tr. H. Rackham and W. H. S. Jones, especially vols 4–6 (LCL, 1950–2) and the revised vol. 7 (1980).

Regimen and *Regimen in Acute Diseases*, both traditionally attributed to Hippocrates. See *Hippocrates* tr. W. H. S. Jones, vols 2 and 4 (LCL, 1923).

There is plenty of information about the food and wine of modern Greece, and some history too, in Rena Salaman's *Greek Food* (2nd edn, London, 1993) and Miles Lambert-Gócs's *The Wines of Greece* (London, 1990). The story of classical Greek food is told in Andrew Dalby's *Siren Feasts: a history of food and gastronomy in Greece* (London, 1995).

The best books on Roman food and wine are in French: Jacques André's *L'Alimentation et la Cuisine à Rome* (2nd edn, Paris, 1981) and André Tchernia's *Le Vin de l'Italie Romaine* (Rome, 1986). Emily Gowers' *The Loaded Table* (Oxford, 1993) brings out the complications of Roman poets' references to food. As a survey of the daily life of Rome nothing has replaced Jérôme Carcopino's *Daily Life in Ancient Rome* (London, 1956, and reprinted). Modern Italian food and wine are surveyed by Elizabeth David in her classic *Italian Food* (revised edn, London, 1979) and by Burton Anderson in *The Wine Atlas of Italy* (London, 1990).

Alan Davidson's *Mediterranean Seafood* (revised edn, London, 1981) is the best source of information in English on the fish of Italian and Greek waters.

Lindsay Allason-Jones is the author of *Women in Roman Britain* (London, 1989), which is full of information on the daily life of this obscure Roman province. Finally those who want to know all there is to know about Roman fish sauce will find it in R. I. Curtis' *Garum and Salsamenta: production and commerce in materia medica* (Leiden, 1991).

We are grateful to the authors of the books listed, which we have ourselves found helpful at various points in the present work.

Quotations and References

INTRODUCTION The philosophy of music and cookery: *Regimen* (attributed to Hippocrates) 1, 18.

RECREATING ANCIENT FOOD The comedy cook: Plautus, *Pseudolus* 810–25. The cook who shares his master's taste: Martial, *Epigrams* 13, 220. Fish sauce: Martial, *Epigrams* 13, 102; recipes, *Geoponica* 20, 46. The fate of silphium: Pliny, *Natural History* 19, 39. Raisin wine: Martial, *Epigrams* 13, 106; Pliny, *Natural History* 14, 80–5; Columella, *On Agriculture* 12, 39.

THE HOMECOMING OF ODYSSEUS Calypso and Odysseus: *Odyssey* 5, 194–201. Alcinous' orchard: *Odyssey* 7, 112–21. 'Never ate a fish': Eubulus 118 (*Epitome of Athenaeus* 25c). Maron's wine: *Odyssey* 9, 204–11; Pliny, *Natural History* 14, 54. Pancakes in Greek poetry: Magnes and Cratinus quoted by Athenaeus 646e, Hipponax quoted by Athenaeus 645c. Circe's *kykeon*: *Odyssey* 10, 233–6. Byzantine scholar on *kykeon*: Archbishop Eustathius of Thessalonica, *Commentary on Homer* 870, 65, compare Plutarch, *Symposium Questions* 7, 1. Carthaginian porridge: Cato, *On Agriculture* 85. *Alphiton*: Dieuches, quoted in Oribasius, *Medical Collections* 4, 6.

THE BANQUET OF PHILOXENUS Philoxenus, *Banquet*: extracts from longer quotations given by Athenaeus at 685d, 146f and 642f. 'Modern scholars': the exception is D. F. Sutton in her *Dithyrambographi Graeci* (Hildesheim, 1989), who, like us, takes Philoxenus of Cythera to be the author. Agathon's symposium: Plato, *Symposium* 176e; 212c-e. Xenophon, *Symposium*. The story of Aristotle's deathbed: Aulus Gellius, *Attic Nights* 13, 5 (with acknowledgements to J. C. Rolfe's translation in the Loeb Classical Library). The later author who liked the wine of Eresus was Galen, *On the Therapeutic Method* 12, 4. Archestratus on *horaion*: Archestratus 38. The curative qualities of cabbage and a recipe for *oxymeli* with salt: Pliny, *Natural History* 20, 81; 23, 60 (from the Greek author Dieuches); Cato, *On Agriculture* 157, 7. The Cornish recipe for barley bread: *Cornish Recipes Ancient and Modern*, compiled by Edith Martin for the Cornwall Federation of Women's Institutes, 5th edn, 1930.

THE MARKETS OF THE MEDITERRANEAN Five months' journey: *Periplus of the Mediterranean* attributed to Scylax. The gifts of Dionysus: Hermippus 63 quoted in the *Epitome of Athenaeus* 27e. The law of Thasos: *IG* XII suppl. 347. The Roman scholar who wrote superciliously of Archestratus' appetites is Athenaeus at 116f. On bonito and on wheat bread: Archestratus 13, 4. On Democritus and grape varieties: Pliny, *Natural History* 14, 20. On Tyrian exports: *Ezekiel* 27, 17–33.

A WEDDING FEAST IN MACEDON Hippolochus, *Letter to Lynceus*: extracts from the longer quotation given by Athenaeus at 128a. Oxyrhynchus cookery book: see *Opsartytika und Verwandtes* ed. F. Bilabel (Heidelberg, 1920). Archestratus on hare: Archestratus 57.

CATO'S FARM On visiting the farm, selling surplus stock, and preserving lentils: Cato, *On Agriculture* 2, 1; 2, 7; 116. Cato's remark on Lucius Veturius: Plutarch, *Cato Major* 9, 6 (with acknowledgements to A. E. Astin's translation in his *Cato the Censor*, Oxford, 1978). On the Opimian vintage and on investment in wine: Pliny, *Natural History* 14, 55; 14, 57. Greek recipe for *plakous*: Antiphanes quoted by Athenaeus 449c.

THE WEALTH OF EMPIRE Farm-fresh dinner menu: Juvenal, *Satires* 11, 56–76. Trimalchio's feast: Petronius, *Satyricon* 31; 34. The priestly dinner: Metellus Pius quoted by Macrobius, *Saturnalia* 3, 13, 10–12. The meal that Septicius Clarus missed: Pliny the Younger, *Letters* 1, 15, 1–4. Fashions in wine: Pliny, *Natural History* 14, 95–7. Greek recipe for *conditum*: *Geoponica* 8, 31 (attributed, implausibly, to Democritus). Vestine cheese and Picentine bread: Pliny, *Natural History* 11, 241; 18, 106.

ON HADRIAN'S WALL Horace at Benevento: Horace, *Satires* 1, 5. The inn advertisement: *CIL* 9, 2689 ('penny' in the translation stands for the Roman copper coin *as*). The day-book: no. 190 in Alan Bowman and J. D. Thomas, *The Vindolanda Writing-Tablets* (London, 1994); *acetum* is here translated 'vinegar', not 'sour wine for soldiers', because of the small quantity. Foods introduced to Britain: see J. Grieg, 'Plant foods in the past' in *Journal of Plant Foods* vol. 5 (1983), pp. 179–214. The flavoured wines of Provence: Pliny, *Natural History* 14, 68. Slicing eggs: Plato, *Symposium* 190d.

SUPPER AT THE BATHS The all-night bars: Juvenal, *Satires* 8, 158–80. Street sounds and smells: Seneca, *Letters* 56, 2. Trimalchio at the baths: Petronius, *Satyricon* 27. The baths of Tigellinus: compare Philostratus, *Life of Apollonius of Tyana* 4, 42. The conversation: *Kathemerine Homilia* attributed to Pollux (ed. A. Boucherie [Paris, 1872]: 'yoghurt' and 'halva' are approximate equivalents only for *colostrum* and *gelonianum*). The wines of Verona: Cassiodorus, *Variae* 12, 4.

142

Index

Page numbers in italic refer to illustrations.

Illustration Acknowledgements

The publishers would like to thank the following for supplying illustrations: The Trustees of the British Museum, London, pages 1, 3, 12, 14, 15, 35, 43, 44, 45, 51, 53, 57, 58, 59, 69, 70, 72, 73, 74, 84, 88, 94, 115, 118, 122; The J. Paul Getty Museum, Malibu 2, 6, 13, 17, 21, 27, 29, 30, 31, 33, 39, 47, 54, 64, 67, 83, 107, 110, 129, 131, 134; Ashmolean Museum, Oxford 11, 71, 139; Bibliothèque Nationale, Paris 22; Mansell Collection, London (Museo Nazionale, Rome) 25; Museum of Antiquities, University of Newcastle upon Tyne 18; Scala Istituto Fotografico Editoriale SpA, Florence (Museo Nazionale, Naples) 23, 87, 99, (Pompeii) 102; Idryma Theras (Thera Foundation) 63; Vatican Museums 61, 77, 93, 105, 116, 120, 121, 125, 127, 133; Martin von Wagner Museum, Universität Würzburg (photo: K. Oehrlein) 79. The line drawing on page 47 is after F. Lissarrague, *Un Flot d'images*, Adam Biro, Paris, 1987, page 70 (Antikensammlungen, Munich); the others are by Sue Bird.